FIRST THEY
TOOK ROME

How the Populist Right Conquered Italy

David Broder

VERSO
London • New York

1 3 5 7 9 10 8 6 4 2

Verso
UK: 6 Meard Street, London W1F 0EG
US: 20 Jay Street, Suite 1010, Brooklyn, NY 11201
versobooks.com

Verso is the imprint of New Left Books

ISBN-13: 978-1-78663-761-1
ISBN-13: 978-1-78663-763-5 (UK EBK)
ISBN-13: 978-1-78663-764-2 (US EBK)

British Library Cataloguing in Publication Data
A catalogue record for this book is available from the British Library

Library of Congress Cataloging-in-Publication Data
A catalog record for this book is available from the Library of Congress

Typeset in Adobe Garamond Pro by Hewer Text UK Ltd, Edinburgh
Printed and bound by CPI Group (UK) Ltd, Croydon CR0 4YY

Contents

Party Acronyms

AN – Alleanza Nazionale (National Alliance; postfascist, 1994–2009)

CDU – Christlich Demokratische Union (Christian Democratic Union; centre-right, 1945–present)

CSU – Christlich-Soziale Union (Christian Social Union; centre-right, 1945–present)

DC – Democrazia Cristiana (Christian Democracy; big tent, 1942–94)

DP – Democrazia Proletaria (Proletarian Democracy; far-left, 1975–91)

DS – Democratici di Sinistra (Democrats of the Left; centre-left, 1998–2007)

FdI – Fratelli d'Italia (Brothers of Italy; postfascist, 2014–present)

FI – Forza Italia (centre-right/Berlusconian, 1994–2009, 2013–present)

IdV – Italia dei Valori (Italy of Values; centre-left, anti-corruption, 1998–present)

LeU – Liberi e Uguali (Free and Equal; centre-left, 2017–present)

M5S– Movimento Cinque Stelle (Five Star Movement; big tent, anti-corruption, 2009–present)

MSI – Movimento Sociale Italiano (Italian Social Movement; neofascist, 1946–95)

NAR – Nuclei Armati Rivoluzionari (neofascist, 1977–81)

NCD – Nuovo Centrodestra (centre-right, 2013–17)

PaP – Potere al Popolo (Power to the People)

PCI – Partito Comunista Italiano (Italian Communist Party, 1921–91)

PD – Partito Democratico (Democratic Party)

PdCI – Partito dei Comunisti Italiani (Party of Italian Communists; communist, 1998—present)

PdL – Popolo della Libertà (People of Freedom, centre-right/Berlusconian, 2009–13)

PDS – Partito Democratico della Sinistra (Democratic Party of the Left; centre-left, 1991–98)

PRC – Partito della Rifondazione Comunista (Communist Refoundation Party; communist, 1991–present)

PSDI – Partito Socialista Democratico Italiano (Italian Democratic Socialist Party; centre-left, 1947–98)

PSI – Partito Socialista Italiano (Italian Socialist Party; centre-left, 1892–1994)

RC – Rivoluzione Civile (Civic Revolution, far-left, anti-corruption, 2013)

SEL – Sinistra Ecologia Libertà (Left Ecology Freedom; centre-left, 2009–16)

SPD – Sozialdemokratische Partei Deutschlands (Social Democratic Party; centre-left, 1875–present)

UU – Uniti nell'Ulivo (United in the Olive Tree; centre-left, 2004–07)

Introduction

As an English resident of Rome, I never cease to hear middle-class Italians singing the praises of a 'normal country' – Britain. Seen from Italy, ours is a land of efficient bus services, friendly locals offering up trays of tea and cakes, and earnest professionalism in public life. When one recent Italian president came under criticism in a wiretapping scandal, the country's leading newspaper lamented the absence of the 'businesslike respect' that supposedly characterises exchanges in the House of Commons.

This isn't the only curious model. As Italy prepared to join the eurozone, one leading editor at *La Repubblica* issued a book entitled *Germanizzazione*, characterising the single currency as a German takeover – but saying this was a good thing. Mario Monti, who became prime minister in 2011, concurred that if Italy was to become a 'normal country' it would require some 'external bind' – what he called 'denying our own selves a little'. What seemed least of all 'normal' in such comments was their obsession with foreign models.

Perhaps we should instead question the idea that Italy is really so unusual. Studies of Italian political history often present it as a patchwork of cultural peculiarities, the anomalous result of late national unification and its position on the periphery of Europe. Yet, in the age of Brexit and Donald Trump, the volatility and fragmentation of Italian public life no longer seem unique. Today, its institutional turmoil is rather less a mark of backwardness and more like a vision of our own future.

Former Trump aide Steve Bannon recognised this in October 2018 when he chose to site his populist academy at a monastery near Rome – what he called the 'centre of the political universe'. He came to Italy to learn from Matteo Salvini, the latest leader to turn the country's politics upside down. After almost three decades in which democratic institutions have withered, Salvini has not just turned his Lega into an all-Italian force but polarised the entire political field around his nationalist agenda.

The last thirty years of turmoil have, indeed, made volatility the new normal in Italian public life. Its parties change names constantly; leading political personnel are prone to outrageous antics; and Italians love to talk about the idiosyncrasies that supposedly make this country beyond comparison. Yet, underneath the noise and colour is a simpler reality – a major industrialised power, with deep-rooted democratic traditions that has, in recent decades, sunk into profound economic stagnation and political tumult.

Some commentators tell us that things were always like this – that Italy was forever backward and dysfunctional, that it never got over fascism, or that this land of 'functional illiterates' has been prey to demagogues ever since Caesar. Yet what is happening today really is new. In the postwar decades, Italy enjoyed such rapid economic growth that it even surpassed British GDP per capita; its anomaly was precisely that it had a permanent party of government as well as the West's largest Communist Party, in opposition.

Yet, if this was the normality even into the 1980s, today the opposite holds true. The Second Republic inaugurated after the end of the Cold War has instead seen one of Europe's best-performing economies turn into among the weakest, with dismal investment, withering infrastructure, and around a third of young people neither in work nor study. This shift is also reflected in political turmoil, with no force able to impose itself in an enduring way.

In the 1990s, many insisted that the modernisation of Italy relied on the 'external bind' provided by the European project. Italy was, at that point, one of the most federalist countries, seduced by the prospect of becoming a 'normal country'. Back then, not only the liberal centre-left but the Lega Nord and Silvio Berlusconi held up the EU as a force that would 'heal' Italy's public finances and improve its political culture. Yet, in 2020, Italians' Euroscepticism today rivals even that of their British counterparts.

Europe can little withstand a mounting climate of Italian disaffection. The third-largest eurozone economy, an Italian default or exit from the single currency would spoke wide-scale turmoil. Yet the necessary relief through debt cancellation would jeopardise the eurozone's most fundamental dogmas. Both Too Big to Fail and Too Big to Save, Italy is instead condemned to a permanent crisis-management regime, outright collapse forever kicked a few months down the road.

There is little appetite for an open break with the euro. Before the 2018 general election, both the Movimento

Cinque Stelle (Five Star Movement; M5S) and the Lega renounced any prospect of leaving the single currency. In recent years, these insurgents have exploited a climate of popular discontent also expressed in Italians' mounting distrust for Brussels. But this political malaise also entails a general loss of faith in great collective endeavours, preventing even these forces from foreseeing a leap into the dark outside the eurozone.

The extreme volatility in Italian politics has come hand-in-hand with the narrowing of political choice. The theatre of personality and identity intensifies, whereas the prospect of a change of economic priorities is abandoned. If even such insurgents as M5S and the Lega speak not of the collective interests of the Italian people, but only of defending the 'ordinary citizen', they seem less to galvanise the masses in a populist revolt as to reflect a pervasive mood of atomised, individual despair.

To explain the volatile times in which these parties have risen to prominence, this book is patterned following the key developments in recent Italian history, from the end of the Cold War to the Berlusconi era and the wake of the 2008 economic crisis. It examines the insurgents' political agenda and forms of mobilisation and how their opponents contrived to provide them a road to power. A study of this national history moreover allows us to identify tensions pulling public life apart across the West.

Chapter 1 explains how the Lega Nord made its first appearance on the political scene. It argues that the collapse of the Cold War order and the destruction of the parties on which it was based opened the door to an assault on democratic standards. Exploiting the anti-corruption mood, the northern-chauvinist Lega allied with other populist forces – from

Silvio Berlusconi to the postfascists – to impose a new 'anti-political' common sense, through which the hard right could push its own cultural tropes.

Chapter 2 looks at the demise of the opposition to these rising reactionary forces – and the collapse of the once-mighty Italian left. In particular, this chapter examines how in the 1990s and 2000s the parties of a 'modernised' centre-left tried – and failed – to change their base, riding the wave of anti-corruption politics, anti-Berlusconism, and the mania for privatisation to reorient toward a liberal Europeanist identity.

Chapter 3 presents Italy as a gerontocracy – a country for old men. In an era in which young people are unable to find work and most are forced to live with their parents, property owners and those with established positions of authority cement their social control. A focus on youth emigration, as well as ministers' rhetoric around the 'lazy', 'choosy' young people unable to make their way in Italy, highlights the sources of youth disillusionment with the political process.

Chapter 4 examines the breakthrough of new political forces harnessing the mood of discontent. It argues that the promise of M5S to smash open Italy's gerontocracy has flipped into a technocratic and depoliticised vision of government, offering the atomised citizen a more rational state administration. Yet the party also draws on a deep welter of mistrust in institutions, with the hollowing-out of public debate, falling voter turnout, and the search for technocratic quick fixes.

The rise of M5S, cannibalising the youth and working-class vote and upending the centre-left, has, in turn, served as a springboard for Matteo Salvini's Lega, notwithstanding this party's very different base of support. Chapter 5 argues that even as the Lega radicalises it is moving closer to a prize unclaimed in decades: the creation of a nation-wide conservative party, integrating traditional elites even in once-inhospitable regions.

We begin with a plunge into Italy's recent history – with the Lega's first arrival on the political scene.

I

The Pole of Good Government

Even before the election was called, the insurgents' antics in the Chamber of Deputies illustrated their rising confidence. As evidence mounted of the former prime minister's criminal ties, one Lega Nord MP even waved a noose at the government benches. And when Italians did pass their verdict at the polls, they issued a withering condemnation of the establishment parties. More than two-thirds of incumbent MPs lost their seats, as an anti-corruption movement founded just three years previously became the biggest party in the Chamber of Deputies. The Lega Nord's venom against the ex-Communist centre-left complemented its war on the bankrupt traditional right, whose MPs it now unseated across the upper part of Italy. Identifying its own electoral offensive with the magistrates' exposal of a vast web of bribes and kickbacks, the northern-chauvinist party promised to impose its radical agenda on a new populist administration.

This isn't a description of Matteo Salvini's breakthrough in 2018, but of a political revolution that took place a quarter century previously. In the 1994 general election, Umberto Bossi's Lega Nord – an alliance of six regional leagues that formed a single force at the end of the 1980s – elected more MPs than any other party, taking 117 seats in the 630-member Chamber of Deputies. Based on 8.5 per cent of the vote, the Lega Nord's tally owed to the geographical concentration of its support – and despite its seat numbers, it entered government as a junior partner in Silvio Berlusconi's coalition. Yet its anti-political sentiment had attracted broad-based support in Italian society, as it united a populist deprecation of political elites with the free-marketeer call for a Thatcherite revolution in Italy. Bossi's party portrayed itself as the voice of the productive, modern North in rebellion against 'thieving Rome' and the 'lazy, corrupt South'.

By 2018, the Lega was a rather different beast – it had become an all-Italian nationalist party, indeed a nationwide challenge to Berlusconi. Yet its success under Salvini's leadership would have been impossible without the fortresses it built in the 1990s. In the 2018 general election, when 50 per cent of all votes went to either the Movimento Cinque Stelle (Five Star Movement; M5S) or the Lega, this was widely characterised in terms of the death of the traditional parties. Even taken together, the centre-left Democrats and Berlusconi's Forza Italia had totalled just 33 per cent of the vote – M5S leader Luigi di Maio could declare the demise of the 'Second Republic' dominated by these forces. Yet a look at the events of 1994 exposes the shallow roots of these 'established' parties – and a longer period of volatility that allowed the populist right to begin its rise. The 2018 general election is easily presented as a unique moment of turmoil, given that 65.9 per cent of incumbent MPs either quit or lost their seats. Yet this was in fact slightly less than the legislative turnover witnessed in 1994 (where 66.8 per cent of MPs were ejected), and similar to that seen in the last contest in 2013 (65.5 per cent).[1]

When we understand this longer period of upheaval we also begin to doubt the suggestion that the M5S–Lega pact sealed in June 2018 represented Europe's 'first all-populist government'.[2] For the anti-political sentiment that is today spreading across the West emerged in Italy not only at the moment of Trump and Brexit, but a quarter century previously. Already back then Italy had seen the destruction of the 'First Republic' that had taken form after World War II, a republic whose parties – the Christian-Democrats (DC), Socialists (PSI) and Communists (PCI) – each reached the end of their respective histories between 1991 and 1994. These parties' disappearance decisively cut the ground from underneath the Italian political system – and prepared the way for its reconstitution on new and less stable bases.

Indeed, if after the M5S's success in the March 2018 general election Di Maio claimed that citizen power had triumphed over 'establishment' parties like the Democratic Party (PD) and Forza Italia, the forces thus swept aside were in fact ephemeral products of the last couple of decades. If in the 1990s these parties reproduced a classic binary between centre-left and centre-right, they also reflected the postmodern times that followed the end of the Cold War, with the demise of the long-prevalent Communist and Catholic political families. These new forces' life has, instead, been marked by radical shifts in the political landscape, from Italy's integration into a new European order to the decline of the labour movement and the hollowing out of the old mass-membership parties. Faced with a seemingly perpetual crisis, a series of saviours have emerged promising to stabilise the state again, from Silvio Berlusconi to former central bankers and even Matteo Renzi. In this sense, Matteo Salvini's Lega is just the latest force that promises to restore order in place of chaos.

The end of the First Republic was no single event – and was shaped by the frailties that had long built up in the Christian-Democratic-dominated state that emerged from World War II. The death of this order in the early 1990s married such developments as the Communist Party's self-dissolution, the felling of the Socialists and Christian Democrats by anti-corruption magistrates, the acceleration of European integration, and the rise of Berlusconism. But as the old party containers collapsed, the Italian political system would have to be founded on new bases – and the forms it took showed just how far the ties between parties and society had weakened. This laid the basis for a new series of political forces – including a radicalised right, breaking from the Christian-Democratic past.

With the death of the forces that had dominated public life since 1945, mass-membership parties gave way to a series of 'saviour' figures from outside the world of politics, as judges, technocrats, and TV performers all promised to drain the swamp of corruption in Rome. The death of the First Republic was not an edifying spectacle – but it certainly was a spectacle. This was visible right from the opening act of its demise, the 'Clean Hands' trials that began in 1992. Exposing the web of kickbacks and embezzlement that had built up under the ancien régime, the trials turned the investigating judges into celebrities, as their cross-examination of leading politicians was beamed into Italians' living rooms. Yet the effect was to feed a deep popular cynicism in political action itself.

Clean Hands began in 1992 not because of some sudden spike in corruption, so much as the destabilisation of Italian politics at the end of the Cold War. This largely owed to the dissolution of the Communist PCI in 1991, a development that had, at first, promised to lower the stakes of political combat. The perceived threat from the Communists – Italy's second-most-powerful party – had long favoured elite connivance, serving both as an enemy to unite against and a reason for the other parties and their media outriders not to delve too deeply into each other's affairs. However, the disappearance of this Communist bogeyman undermined the historic solidarity between Italian elites and parties like the Catholic DC and the soft-left PSI, which immediately came under intense scrutiny. But if the PCI's historic rivals now felt freer to start throwing mud at one another, this did not leave public life any cleaner. Rather, the destruction of the old mass parties opened the way to forces that even more blatantly conflated public and private interests.

This was epitomised by media tycoon Silvio Berlusconi, who entered the political stage in 1994. His project was to recreate the Right around his own person, while also exploiting the wider atmosphere of deregulation and liberalisation. He galvanized his base with vehement attacks on 'Reds' and 'communists' – the centre-left in turn denounced Berlusconi's vulgar personal conduct and debasement of public life. Yet many of their ideological assumptions were surprisingly similar. In 1991, the Communist Party had, as if apologetically, changed its name to Democratic Party of the Left; the former adepts of Lenin and Antonio Gramsci soon styled themselves not as partisans of labour but as the aspiring managers of a lean, clean, and pro-business institutional machine. It would in coming years repeatedly lend its parliamentary support to technocratic administrations, even appointing unelected central bank administrators as ministers in its own governments. Under the powerful influence of the Communist and Socialist left, the Constitution promulgated in 1947 had declared Italy a 'democratic republic founded on labour' – putting an at least rhetorical emphasis on the interests of working people. In its liberalised, 1990s form, the centre-left instead altered the Constitution to entrench balanced budgets and sobriety in the public accounts.

The First Republic had been no golden age, and its ignominious downfall was no conspiracy. As journalist Marco Travaglio summarily put it, the trials which exposed Bribesville took place 'because there had been a lot of bribes'. Yet, as Eric Hobsbawm said of the dissolution of the Communist Party, the effect of breaking up the mass parties was in many ways to 'throw out the baby and keep the bathwater',[3] replacing corruption-ridden parties with personalised forces whose internal affairs were even more inscrutable. Far from strengthening Italian democracy, the destruction of the First Republic instead opened the way for a wholesale attack on the institutional and cultural inheritance of postwar Italy, from employment rights to anti-fascism and even the role of the Constitution itself. Indeed, the greater effect of the wave of anti-political sentiment was not to hand power back to ordinary citizens, but rather to prepare the way for reactionary, privatising, and even criminal forces able to exploit the void at the heart of public life. The 'liberal revolution' promised by the parties of the Second Republic would, in fact, prepare the perfect breeding ground for the Lega.

Addio, Prima Repubblica

The idea of numbering republics might seem rather strange – indeed, it is the invention of Italian journalists, seeking to delimit changes of the political times, rather than part of the state's official name. This habit comes from across the Alps, where France is today on its 5ème République. In that country, four other republics have surged and crashed since the monarchy was first felled by the French Revolution. These states' history has, on each occasion, been bracketed by crises in France's place in the international order, whether due to the threat of invasion (1793), military defeat (1870, 1940, 1958), or revolution across the European continent (1848). These upheavals each brought a different constitutional regime that proposed to impose order over tumult – on three such occasions, the new republic came after a period of restored monarchical rule or foreign occupation. In Italy, the transitions from First to Second and Third Republic entailed no such violent breaks, or even constitutional change. But in each instance, the power sharing between the main parties ended in their collective collapse, and the rise of a new party system framed by different ideological imperatives.

Like their French counterparts, Italy's republics have tended to stand or fall based on the country's international position. The First Republic emerged from the fall of Mussolini's empire, and its politics were essentially determined by the Cold War divide, first visible in the competing influences of the US–UK armies and mostly left-wing elements of the Resistance that had helped free Italy from Nazi–Fascist rule. In postwar months, the main forces that had gathered in the National Liberation Committee (the DC, the PCI, and the Socialist PSIUP) together wrote a new democratic constitution, bearing a spirit of progress and anti-fascist unity. Yet, already before the document was enacted, DC premier Alcide de Gasperi's spring 1947 visit to the United States augured a political realignment. Returning bolstered by promises of Marshall Plan investment, he kicked the PCI and PSIUP out of the ruling coalition, leaving his own party as the pivot of all future governments.

Hopes that the Resistance would drive a deep renovation of Italian institutions were rapidly thwarted. The House of Savoy's attempts to backslide from its two-decade pact with Benito Mussolini were not enough to save it in the June 1946 referendum, when Italians narrowly voted to abolish the monarchy. Yet the immediate postwar years brought an amnesty for most Fascist-era crimes, thanks to legislation authored by PCI leader and erstwhile Justice Minister Palmiro Togliatti in the name of restoring social peace. Just 1,476 of 143,871 Fascist-era officials examined by the purges commission were removed from their posts.[4] At the same time, the myth of a unanimous national Resistance had the perverse effect of avoiding a reckoning with the past, not only sealing the legitimacy of the partisan minority but also exculpating the passive-to-collaborationist mass. After the end of the Resistance coalition in 1947, it was, instead, the Communists themselves who came most under scrutiny.

The end of the war and the economic 'miracle' of the 1950s and 1960s were a moment of rapid industrialisation with few parallels in Europe, feeding optimism that Italy was leaving the bad old days behind it. Its stagnant institutional politics nonetheless lagged behind the many other modernising drives within Italian society. This particularly owed to the dominance of the DC. Not only could the party count

on a solid base in the Catholic middle classes and rural South
– guaranteeing it 35–40 per cent of the popular vote in each
general election – but it enjoyed a US-backed stranglehold
over the national institutions, as Italian NATO membership
effectively forbade ministerial roles being entrusted to the
PCI. Yet the DC did not have everything its own way. Its
1950s bid to legislate an automatic majority for the largest
party was thwarted by smaller parties, and subsequent
decades of coalition rule were marked by a constant balancing act between the *democristiani*'s internal factions and various minor-party allies.

This system faced a first major test in 1960, with an
episode that threatened to bring the neofascist Movimento
Sociale Italiano (Italian Social Movement; MSI) into the
mainstream. In the 1950s, this party founded by Mussolini
nostalgists had drifted from anti-American and rhetorically
anti-capitalist positions toward the search for alliance with
DC hardliners, in which vein it gave its outside backing to
two *democristiano* cabinets in the late 1950s. In 1960, when
the Partito Socialista Democratico Italiano (Italian Social-
Democratic Party, a party of anti-communist social democrats) pulled out of their alliance with the Catholic centre
party, the DC was left without a majority in parliament;
appointed prime minister on 26 March 1960, the DC's
Fernando Tambroni thus formed a cabinet reliant on neofascist votes. Though the MSI was offered no ministerial roles,
the signs of its emboldening – and its provocative bid to
hold its congress in anti-fascist Genoa – sparked widespread
opposition and even rioting. Over summer 1960, some
eleven people were killed by police during anti-MSI protests.

However, this crisis ultimately served to marginalise the
far right. The instability that Tambroni had fostered soon

provoked a revolt among DC grandees, and by July they had forced him out of office, never to return to alliance with the MSI. Instead, the movement stretching from the industrial North to the Mafia-plagued farms of the South marked the onset of a class revolt not seen since the Resistance, which also helped impose a wider *cordon sanitaire* against the neofascists. Wary of further such disturbances coming from the left wing of the political spectrum, more liberal elements of the DC instead decided the time was right to integrate the Socialists into the so-called *centrosinistra* pact, in a 'modernising' arrangement that both preserved and renewed the DC's central role to all coalition-making. Only in the 1980s would the DC hand the prime minister's job to the centrist Republicans and later the Socialists; it in all cases remained the dominant force in each cabinet.

The constant coalition-making was weakly responsive to electoral pressure. As journalist Paolo Mieli has noted, since national unification in 1861 the Italian electorate has only been able to impose a direct exchange of power between Left and Right twice (in 1996 and 2008), and it did not do so once during the First Republic (1948–92).[5] The constant rise in the Communist vote from 1948 onward (first set back only in 1979) instead drew the other parties into closer cooperation. Able to treat the Italian state as if it were their own property in a 'blocked democracy', they operated on the basis of the Cencelli system, so named after a *democristiano* functionary who proposed dividing up ministries and public posts among party factions according to size, on the model of shareholders. This allowed them to share out not only government jobs but also control of tendering processes and influence over state agencies like public broadcaster Radiotelevisione italiana (RAI), on the basis of interparty agreements.

This cartelisation reached its peak in the 1980s, as the governments of the *pentapartito* alliance brought smaller and weaker rooted parties into institutional power-sharing. This five-party administration included all the main parliamentary forces except the Communists and neofascists and, in 1983, allowed the appointment, for the first time, of a Socialist prime minister – Bettino Craxi. The *pentapartito* epitomised the way in which the First Republic's dominant forces could divide up posts and influence among themselves, indeed increasingly becoming factions integrated into the sharing of institutional power, rather than mass-membership parties. Craxi's tenure marked a notable shift to the right for the Socialist Party, which both renounced its historic ties to Marxism and more sharply distanced itself from Enrico Berlinguer's PCI. Yet he would enter the collective memory less as a heretic on the left than an embodiment of the corruption that brought the First Republic to its knees.

We have noted that Italy's republics have tended to stand or fall based on the country's international position. The end of the First Republic especially owed to the end of the Cold War, in particular insofar as the collapse of the Eastern Bloc served as the trigger for the dissolution of the PCI. Later, we will look more closely at the PCI's demise and the consequences this had for the broader Italian left. Its immediate effect, however, was to undermine the solidarity on the other side of the political spectrum, among forces long cohered by their anti-communism. In autumn 1990 came revelations of Gladio, the so-called 'stay-behind operation' that NATO had developed in order to prepare military resistance to a PCI coup or Soviet invasion. When President Francesco Cossiga, in one of his characteristic outbursts, openly admitted his role in Gladio, the left-wing parties demanded his impeachment, soon forcing his resignation. Yet as Cossiga himself noted, once the Berlin Wall had fallen, the forces 'pushing from the other side' – notably the DC – were not going to be left standing either.[6]

The downfall of the old edifice began in 1992 with the arrest of the Socialist Mario Chiesa, a leading light in the Milan PSI. As administrator of the city's Pio Albergo Trivulzio nursing home, Chiesa received tens of millions of lire in kickbacks from the cleaning company boss Luca Magni in exchange for contracts. When Magni, unable to withstand the mounting payments, finally reported the situation to the magistrate Antonio di Pietro, a sting operation was set in motion against the corrupt machine politician. On the early evening of 17 February, Magni entered Chiesa's office with a secret microphone and camera; when the Socialist agreed to the transaction, as expected, the *carabinieri* burst into the room. Alarmed, Chiesa bolted into the toilet with the 37 million lire (about €20,000) in cash from another bribe, which he then attempted, in vain, to hide in the cistern. As the news spread across the TV networks, party boss Bettino Craxi tried to dismiss Chiesa as a 'lone crook': the Milan PSI, in the nation's 'moral capital' was, after all run by 'honest people'.

Not all were convinced. Already in a May 1991 article for Milan magazine *Società civile*, the magistrate Di Pietro had written of a mounting climate of impunity – in his view, public tendering should be characterised

> less in terms of corruption or abuse of office than an environment of illegal payments, an objective situation in which those who have to pay no longer even wait to be

asked for it, knowing that in this climate bribes and pay-offs are customary.[7]

As far back as 1974, the *scandali dei petroli* had exposed the corrupt dealings between oil company bosses and leading politicians. But what more dramatically broke the political system apart in 1992 was its loss of internal solidarity. Cast off by his party and thrown in jail, Chiesa soon began to talk, revealing the vast web of bribe money that the PSI had orchestrated. As the 'Milan pool' judges picked up the men he named, a domino effect developed, and party underlings informed on others to save themselves. Of 4,520 people investigated in Milan, 1,281 were convicted, 965 through plea bargains.

Tearing through the webs of connivance within the old party machines, the Clean Hands process was marked by a robust judicial activism. As judge Francesco Saverio Borrelli said of the politicians investigated, 'we imprison them to make them talk. We let them go after they speak'. However, the spectacle surrounding the cases and the magistrates' rise to public prominence fed their own direct integration into the political field itself. The televised cross-examinations, and especially Di Pietro's brusque tones in the courtroom, upended the First Republic's characteristic etiquette, as stuffy institutional obfuscators were confronted by the crusading spirit of the prosecutor. This was also complemented by a kind of mob justice driven by media, not least as some of those on trial began to hurl muck at one another. When the Milan pool judges began a trial of local officials from the post-Communist Partito Democratico della Sinistra (Democratic Party of the Left; PDS), Lega leader Umberto Bossi proudly marched his supporters into the courtroom to shake Di Pietro's hand before the cameras. The Lega leader himself soon admitted receiving massive illicit sums from the Montedison industrial group.

The image of the strident prosecutor-saviour, exposing the failings of a moribund party system on behalf of cheated Italians, was particularly brought into relief by the government's feeble response. In a clumsy bid to slow the tide of arrests, on 5 March 1993 the administration led by PSI premier Giuliano Amato issued the Decreto Conso, which sought to turn 'illicit party financing' from a criminal to an administrative offense. This decree moreover contained a 'silent clause', which would effectively have allowed it to apply retroactively, thus cutting short thousands of Clean Hands investigations. The Milan pool judges responded with a televised address warning the public of what this really meant, and amid the ensuing uproar the president refused to sign off the government's text. Instead, the political crisis deepened, with news on 27 March that the Palermo public prosecutor was investigating one of the First Republic's linchpins, former DC premier and long-time minister Giulio Andreotti, for Mafia ties. The party system was being brought to its knees.

The malaise spread across partisan divides – and fed calls for a change in the forms of politics. This was particularly expressed in criticism of party lists – the electoral system by which candidates favoured by party machines could be guaranteed election to parliament. An institutional referendum on 18 April saw more than four-fifths of voters back a new system, favouring first-past-the-post contests more akin to the US and UK systems. With 75 per cent of seats distributed on such a basis, the new *Mattarellum* law promised to hand voters direct control over individual officials at the local level. Yet the sitting parliament remained under control of the established parties, and even after Amato's government resigned on 21 April, the Chamber of Deputies was in self-preservation mode. On 29 April, a lower house over half of whose members were under judicial investigation voted to shield Craxi from prosecution. The editor of *La Repubblica*, Italy's leading daily, called it the darkest day in postwar history – when the PSI leader appeared outside Rome's Hotel Raphael, he was angrily confronted by coin-throwing demonstrators shouting 'Why don't you take this, too?' Craxi's reply was simply to accuse rivals of hypocrisy – in decades past, after all, the PCI had taken money from Moscow. But the First Republic, too, was about to go the same way as the Eastern Bloc states.

TV Populism

The April 1992 general election, held just weeks after Mario Chiesa's rush to the toilet, came too early to be determined by Clean Hands. The big losers were, in fact, the heirs to the Communist Party, reeling from both the break-up of the PCI and a wider liberal triumphalism surrounding the demise of the Soviet Union. The first real sign of the post–Clean Hands political dynamics instead came with the local elections held in June and November 1993, where, for the first time, Italians directly elected city mayors. The Christian-Democrats were everywhere defeated, securing only 12 per cent of the votes cast in the capital; the dominant party here was instead the post-Communist PDS, which took Rome and Naples as well as backing the winning candidate in Turin. Yet the most remarkable news came in Milan, where the Lega Nord romped to victory, and with the advances for the postfascist MSI. This far-right party made the run-offs in both Rome (where it took 47 per cent in the second round) and Naples, where Alessandra Mussolini garnered 44 per cent of the vote. If the elections most of all saw the old government parties punished, the second-round *ballottaggi* had also shown conservatives' willingness to rally behind even postfascist candidates to block the PDS.

This also heralded a wider realignment on the right wing of Italian politics. Indeed, if the PDS scored major local successes, the collapse of Christian Democracy was also opening the way for other forces – not just those carrying forth the message of Clean Hands, but also those who sought to put a stop to it. This was particularly evident in the intervention of one of Craxi's long-standing allies, the billionaire TV entrepreneur Silvio Berlusconi. Long an associate but not a member of the PSI, his allegiances instead lay with the Propaganda Due masonic lodge, a fraternity that united mainstream politicians with mob bosses and far-right terrorists. Having come under investigation for his ties to organised crime – and faced with a likely PDS victory in the coming general election – the tycoon sought an immunity for himself rather like that which Craxi had briefly secured. On 26 January 1994, Berlusconi issued a televised address announcing that he himself would 'enter the field' (*scendere in campo*) in the attempt to save Italy from 'the Communists'. The general election called for 27 and 28 March would represent his first test at the ballot box.

The televised address that Berlusconi made from his office on 26 January 1994 was a striking intervention in public debate – Antonio Gibelli estimates that by the end of that evening some 26 million Italians had watched the speech, in whole or in part.[8] But the entrepreneur's decision to take to the field – and particularly his way of presenting it – also augured a new era in Italian politics, characterised by the cult of the reticent popular hero. In his address, the billionaire cast himself as a humble son of Italy who had only reluctantly entered public life, unwilling as he was to live 'in an illiberal country governed by men [the former Communists] double-bound to an economically and politically bankrupt past'.[9] Berlusconi made ample reference to both his business experience and his newness to public life, an 'anti-political' message strengthened by his invocation of the needs of *gente comune* ('ordinary folks') rather than the more cohesive *popolo*. Berlusconi called for an end to party politics, a new era in which Italy would be governed by 'wholly new men' – his would be a 'free organisation of voters' – rather than the 'umpteenth party or faction'. As against the 'cartel of the forces of the Left' (deemed 'orphans of, and nostalgics for, communism'), he called for a 'pole of freedoms' to unite private enterprise and 'love of work' with the family values of Catholic Italy.[10]

The folksier tones of this message fed on a popular loss of faith in institutional elites. Yet Berlusconi's message also called for a stop to the turbulence created by Clean Hands, here coded as a return to 'calm'. He portrayed the PDS in terms of militancy and disruption, indeed in the most classically anti-Communist terms, accusing the party of seeking 'to turn the country into a fulminating street protest [*piazza*], which shouts, rants, condemns'. While Berlusconi pointed to the failings of the 'old political class', he smoothed over the specifics of Bribesville, instead collapsing it into the triptych of 'criminality, corruption and drugs' and the high public debt run up in recent years. The problem, it seemed, was not the actual parties of government, but rather 'politics' as such, from 'the Left' to the 'prophets and saviours' whom the trials had brought to the surface. What could, however, 'make the state work' was a businessman of broad experience. Given this enthusiasm for putting business values into politics, it was no surprise that his candidates in 1994 were dominated by employees of his Fininvest and Publitalia companies.

This regeneration of the right would have been impossible without Berlusconi's pre-existing political ties. Indeed, his media power, rooted in privatisations that had begun in the late 1970s, also owed specifically to his association with the corrupt Socialist prime minister Craxi. Under the First Republic, the public broadcaster RAI had held a monopoly on national television, but this was chipped away over the 1970s with the granting of licenses to supposedly 'local' stations like Berlusconi's Telemilano, which, in reality, broadcast nationally. Already by 1983, his channels sold more ad space than the RAI, and after a legal challenge in 1984–85, Craxi issued the so-called *decreti Berlusconi* to put a formal end to the monopoly. Where RAI was governed by the demands of public-service broadcasting, the tycoon's stations instead served up a diet of escapism, promoting the sovereignty of the consumer and a Gordon Gekko–style image of success. The tacky glamour promoted by prime-time chat and US soaps was allied to the carefree materialism of the game show. Some, like comedian Beppe Grillo (cast out by RAI after his trashing of Craxi), refused to appear on the billionaire's channels. But Berlusconi had a platform to address tens of millions.

In this sense, it soon became clear that the judicial offensive against 'the parties' had opened the way to powerful and well-structured forces even less democratic than their First

Republic predecessors. Berlusconi's Forza Italia vehicle – a creation of his media empire in which he personally picked the candidates – had neither local branches, members, party congresses or internal elections. In the 1994 general election it was also allied to other radical forces, from Umberto Bossi's Lega Nord to Gianfranco Fini's MSI (now rebadged Alleanza Nazionale, National Alliance; AN). These parties like Berlusconi each vaunted their credentials as 'outsiders' who stood against the political legacy of the First Republic. Yet, in truth, they merely represented different souls of the Right. While Berlusconi's televised address had augured a Thatcher-style revolution in Italy ('liberal in politics, free-marketeer in economics'), this stood at odds with the more paternalist hues of the AN and small centrist forces; the Lega Nord, based in the heartlands of the wartime Resistance, in turn refused to enter any direct alliance with the postfascists.

Berlusconi's coalition soon took a lead in the polls – trashing any hopes that Clean Hands might have paved the centre-left's own path to high office. And the result of the March 1994 election was the destruction of the parties that had ruled Italy since World War II. The right-wing coalitions built around Forza Italia amassed some 16.6 million votes, as the candidates of Berlusconi, Bossi, and Fini drew almost 43 per cent support. This was a massive blow for the PDS, whose Alliance of Progressives scored just 13.3 million votes (34 per cent); the surviving trunks of the old DC, a party that had been the largest party of government without interruption from 1944 to 1992, won the backing of only 6.1 million Italians, less than 16 per cent of the total. Aside from the sheer speed of the new right's breakthrough, the result was also remarkable for the distribution of seats. Held under the new electoral law[11] passed by referendum in April

1993 – with 75 per cent of seats assigned on the basis of first-past-the-post – the March 1994 contest made the Lega the largest single party in the Chamber of Deputies and gave Berlusconi and his allies a hundred-seat majority, though they fell marginally short in the Senate.

Rehabilitating the Far Right

Such a rapid electoral triumph was impressive for a man who claimed that he had 'never wanted to enter politics'. Indeed, this claim pointed not only to Berlusconi's 'outsider' status, but also his opportunism in entering the public arena. From the start of his reign, it was obvious that he had sought high office in order to shield himself from fraud and racketeering charges, both exploiting the political chaos created by Clean Hands and trying to protect himself from it. The Biondi bill of July 1994 – a bid to put an end to Clean Hands, ultimately felled by the Lega (after some equivocation) – was a first, failed, example of the *ad personam* legislation that Berlusconi used to shield himself and his underlings from prosecution. Where the old parties' local sections, internal elections, and congresses had been *polluted* by conflicts of interest, Forza Italia was *overtly* a web of business associates personally dependent on Berlusconi's empire. At the same time, while the tycoon took his distance from the mass parties of the First Republic, he also took sharply different attitudes to the two forces that had been excluded from high office – the Communists and the neofascists.

When Berlusconi heralded the end of the Cold War as the triumph of liberal values, this looked a lot like a shift to the right, indeed a throwback to a previous age of anti-communism. Indeed, whereas he characterised his own right-wing coalition as 'liberal and Christian', anyone who opposed it was labelled a 'communist'. The neofascist MSI had long claimed that the state, the universities, and public television were overrun with Communists; this same myth was now used by Berlusconi to smear anyone who challenged his interests. For the billionaire, the PDS, the magistrates, and his critics at *The Economist* were part of one same 'Red' establishment: he even labelled this weekly spigot of free-marketeer liberalism *The Ecommunist*. Curiously, the dissolution of the actually existing Communist Party allowed Berlusconi to apply this label all the more indiscriminately. In 2003, he staged a photo op brandishing a fifty-year-old copy of *l'Unità* with the headline 'Stalin Is Dead', cocking a snook at the supposedly 'real' sympathies of his opponents.

Berlusconi's crude re-assertion of anti-communism was also the basis for the rehabilitation of the far right, the 'post-fascists' who joined his so-called Pole of Good Government. As the 1960 attempt to create a Christian-Democratic government reliant on neofascist parliamentary support had shown, the *cordon sanitaire* against the MSI had never been a direct product of the ban on the Fascist Party, but rather owed to mobilised opposition. Over the 1970s, the MSI had remained Italy's fourth largest party, winning up to 9 per cent in national elections; atrocities like the 2 August 1980 bombing of Bologna station, killing eighty-five people, also illustrated the violent threat from more militant neofascist circles around the edges of the MSI. In the 1990s, however, with the demise of the DC, the old *camerati* moved to adopt its positions as their own. At a party congress in 1987, MSI leader Gianfranco Fini had declared himself a 'fascist for the 2000s'; by the time of the 1994 election, he had become the self-proclaimed 'conservative' leader of the new AN.

The ignominious collapse of the DC, combined with the lack of any mass party of the right, presented the space in which longtime fascists could reinvent themselves as a traditional conservative ally of the more 'free-marketeer' Forza Italia. Fini's AN sought closer ties with the small ex-DC factions that had entered the right-wing coalition and also adopted more liberal positions regarding both the European project and immigration (which were now each accepted, but conditionally). This was a break from the MSI's tradition – after all, its roots in the wartime Salò Republic and Mussolini's rearguard struggle against both the Resistance and the US Army had imbued the party with a foundational hostility to the First Republic, and some currents within its ranks such as that led by Pino Rauti had maintained an 'anti-systemic' stance against NATO and European integration. In the 1990s, the AN however eschewed this 'militant' past, creating a socially conservative and pro-European party akin to Spain's post-Franco Partido Popular.

With Berlusconi ready to admit that 'Mussolini did good things, too', the MSI's leaders could wind down their obsession with Il Duce without having to repudiate their own roots entirely. The example of former MSI youth chief Gianni Alemanno, a key architect of the new centre-right, was telling. In 1986, the young fascist had been arrested for attempting to disrupt a ceremony in Nettuno, at which Ronald Reagan honoured the US troops who fell on Italian soil in World War II. Yet, by the time he was elected mayor of the capital in 2008, Alemanno was embarrassed to find his victory greeted by fascist-saluting skinheads outside city hall. He responded with an apparent gesture of contrition, paying a visit to Rome's synagogue in which he extolled the 'universal' values of the fight against Nazism. Yet this was also a means to paint the anti-fascist element of the partisan war as a form of sectarianism: Alemanno decried the 'crimes committed by both sides' in the 'civil war' among Italians.

This relativist offensive against anti-fascist norms made progress in an era in which 'politics' had become a dirty word and in which the Resistance generation were ever less central to public life. There had always been revisionist narratives of Italy's wartime history, seeking to put partisans and fascists on a more equal footing: but only after the fall of the First Republic did they became part of the common sense. This was particularly notable in the success of such works as the novelised 'histories' written by journalist Giampaolo Pansa. His series of works, beginning at the turn of the millennium invoked the 'memory of the defeated' – the silenced and calumnied defenders of Salò – as against the mythology with which the First Republic had garlanded itself.[12] More broadly, revisionist narratives focused on the killings of Italian citizens by Yugoslav partisans, in the so-called foibe massacres; interest in this neighbouring country did not however extend to the far-greater numbers of Yugoslavs slaughtered by Italian troops. The purpose was a domestic, political one, in the bid to undermine anti-fascists' claims to superior moral and democratic standing.

It seemed that the collapse of the old party order had brought a sudden rewriting of its origin story. Indeed, this offensive especially exploited the discredit into which the parties of the Resistance had now fallen. As *il manifesto*'s Lucio Magri put it, after the Bribesville scandal, the democratic republic born of 1945 was no longer bathed in heroism but damned 'as the home of bribes and a party regime that had excluded citizens'; the largest Resistance party, the PCI, was remembered only as 'Moscow's fifth column' therein.[13] This narrative was even taken up by many who had long laboured in its own ranks. Exemplary was Giorgio Napolitano, who joined the PCI in December 1945 and embraced Stalinist orthodoxy before becoming a key leader of the party's most moderate *migliorista* (gradualist) wing. In the 1990s, he sharply repudiated the party's record, which he recast as a regime of lies unable to face up to its own essential criminality. As president from 2006, Napolitano went so far as to commemorate the Communist partisans' victims in the *foibe* of north-eastern Italy, including known fascists.

The Lega Nord

Some anti-fascists did remain mobilised, unwilling to swallow the more flagrant misrepresentations of the republic's founding values. This was visible as early as 25 April 1994, in the commemorations which marked the traditional anniversary of Italy's liberation from Nazi–Fascist rule. When Lega leader Umberto Bossi attempted to join the Liberation Day march in Milan, just four weeks after he had helped elect the most right-wing government in decades, he was quickly driven away by protestors. The Lega Nord was not itself of Mussolinian origin: rooted in the Northern regions where the Resistance was strongest, it expressed a sometimes virulent hostility to Fini's ex-MSI, refusing to seal any direct electoral alliance with the postfascists even when both parties were joined to Berlusconi's Forza Italia. The Lega Nord leader later received a suspended jail sentence after an outburst when he suggested that his members might go 'door to door' and deal with the fascists 'like the partisans did'. Yet Bossi's initial promise that he would 'never' join a government that included postfascists proved short-lived.

Bossi's ability to shift on such a profound question of political identity points to the highly contradictory and opportunistic character of the party he created, as volatile as the political times in which it came to prominence. Its origins lay in the late 1970s, when, spurred by the creation of regional governments, new parties took form in the wealthiest parts of Italy to demand more funds for their own regions. In the 1987 general election, Bossi was elected senator for the Lega Lombarda – a force active in the region surrounding Milan – and, in 1989, it merged with similar groups that had arisen in five other regions, united by a common decentralising agenda. A breakthrough in the 1990 local elections (where the Lega came second-place across Lombardy) showed that it was a force to be reckoned with, and in particular its ability to break through the class binary which had done so much to structure the First Republic's political system. In 1991, the various leagues formed a single party, though, in some contexts, they also maintained their own regional names.

The leagues had made their first advances in regions that had once loyally voted for the DC. Key was a first breakthrough in Veneto, a strongly Catholic region of particular cultural idiosyncrasies, which had long enjoyed an outsized representation in DC cabinets. In the 1950s, this agricultural northeastern region was as poor as southern Italy and marked by similarly high emigration, but its rapid industrialisation over subsequent decades transformed it into the richest part of Italy.[14] Yet as Veneto raced ahead, the local DC led by Antonio Bisaglia was accused of channelling the region's taxes toward an overbearing central state, making local firms pay for its handouts in the less successful south. Where Bisaglia toyed with the notion of creating an autonomous party akin to Bavaria's Christlich-Soziale Union, some local DC cadres went further, in 1979 forming the regionalist Liga Veneta. Building its profile over the 1980s, the Liga would soon exploit the crisis of the First Republic, coming second to the DC in Veneto in the 1992 general election.

Indeed, if the decline of the First Republic presented a vacuum, some 'outsider' forces caught the mood of the time better than others. In an insightful article remarking on the Lega's early breakthroughs, Ilvo Diamanti highlights its capacities as a 'political entrepreneur' – a force which captures and mobilises the disillusionment with some other party, before using this base to conquer a broader popular hegemony.[15] Both the Liga Veneta and Bossi's Lega Lombarda at first saw particular success in areas long held by the Christian-Democrats but where the social glue provided by the Catholic Church was undermined by secularisation. This, however, also corresponded to a changing approach to public life, less defined by unifying cultural visions or even collective material demands, as by a transactional relationship between the atomised citizen and the state. This shift also had a particular class basis – indeed, the leagues were at first heavily based among (mostly male) small businessmen and their employees, categories in which the Lega still enjoys relatively high support. But as the Lega Nord became a more recognised political force, its identitarian appeal became more transversal – and its demography more representative of the areas where it is rooted.[16]

Because its rise has broadly coincided with the decline of the old left – allowing it to win elections even in historic 'red heartlands' – the Lega Nord is often erroneously presented as a 'welfare-chauvinist' party, namely one which claims that reducing migrant numbers is necessary in order to protect and extend the welfare state. Yet, despite its attacks on spending on migrants, the Lega Nord was from the outset also dominated by anti-statism and the call for sharp tax cuts. At its founding congress in 1991, Bossi explicitly connected his regionalism to the simmering discontent against the First Republic and its so-called 'elephantiasis'. The Lega's ability to transcend a purely middle-class electorate owed not so much to the promise of welfare as to the fact that it presented corruption as a characteristically 'southern' problem from which northerners of all classes could be liberated. Bossi told his followers that it was no surprise that the voter revolt against the First Republic had arisen 'in the areas of industrial civilisation, where citizens' relation to institutions is more critical – though it will come in the South too'.[17] Indeed, even before the Bribesville revelations, the Lega was advancing much of what soon became the common sense about Italy's institutions and in particular the need to break the power of a high taxation, a corrupt state machine weighed down by patronage, and clientelism.

The end of the First Republic had raised the importance of 'anti-corruption' in a contradictory and limited way. Contra the Lega's own presentation, both the case of the Milan PSI and Bossi's own behaviour shed doubt on whether abuses could be pinpointed to the South specifically. Indeed, if the Lega Nord's path to prominence was eased by the demise of the old parties, it immediately moved to claim the same privileges – and more illicit benefits – available to its predecessors. In March 1993 Bossi marched his supporters into a Milan courtroom to shake hands with prosecutor Antonio Di Pietro, congratulating him for his moves against the local post-Communist PDS. However, within just months Bossi was himself in the firing line, as a fresh set of hearings – the Enimont trial – exposed the bribes that chemicals giant Montedison had made to figures across the political spectrum: Bettino Craxi, local DC members, and also the Lega leader. Appearing in court at the turn of 1994, Bossi admitted he had illicitly received money from the firm but insisted that he had provided nothing in return.

That Bossi survived this setback provided an early indication that the 'anti-corruption' on which the Lega Nord thrived wasn't just about the kind of wrongdoing that could be tested in court. His party instead used this term as a more nebulous – and conventionally right-wing – attack on unearned reward and state profligacy, as exemplified by the invocation of poor southern regions leeching off the productive North. In this sense, the assault on corruption also adopted a curiously racialised dimension. At the Lega's founding congress in 1991, Bossi explicitly described the party as 'ethno-nationalist' and labelled southerners – pejoratively termed *terroni* – as feckless layabouts to be identified with Arabs or Albanians rather than white Europeans.[18] This cult of the industrious North was also married to a kind of folk nationalism, albeit one limited to certain regions. This party of industrial modernity adopted as its logo the sword-wielding figure of Alberto da Giussano, a mythical warrior who supposedly defended the Carroccio (a four-wheeled war altar) against Frederick Barbarossa in the Battle of Legnano in 1176.

The foundational clash with the First Republic (and indeed the PSI) assumed a lasting place in Lega folklore – as would the party's nickname, the Carroccio. The Lega's sense of territorial rootedness is especially bound to Pontida, a town of 3,000 people near Bergamo, in its Lombardian heartlands, where it made one of its earliest local election successes, during the final years of the First Republic. Responding to the Lega Nord's breakthrough, PSI leader Bettino Craxi paid a visit to the town on 3 March 1990 in which he tried to pander to *leghista* themes, acknowledging the popular demand for a more federal Italy. Unimpressed, local Lega Nord activists jeered the former premier, and three weeks later Bossi and his comrades held their own opposing summit in Pontida. After their massive gains in the 1992 general election, the Lega faithful again met there for a three-day celebration. This set the precedent for a summer festival that continues to this day at which crowds of mostly white-haired Lega activists convene to consume rather grim quantities of meat and beer.

The ritualised return to Pontida typified the party's roots in provincial northern Italy. Contrary to the general tendency of political forces in Italy and beyond, over the 1990s and 2000s, to replace territorial branches with media campaign vehicles, the Lega Nord built its initial rise on cadre structures rather reminiscent of the old mass parties. These were particularly important in ensuring its visible organisation presence even in small communities. Indeed, though the party was from the outset a recipient of funds from the great industrial groups of the North, the Lega Nord's electoral rise was driven not by wealthy urban populations – as heralded by some former Marxists who hailed the liberation of 'dynamic' northern Italy from the 'backward' South – but, rather, by the small towns and hinterlands surrounding these same cities. While it would capture the largest regional governments in northern Italy in 2010, the Lega has in fact never occupied the mayor's office in such major urban centres as Turin, Genoa, Venice, Trieste, Bologna, or Brescia. If, amidst the collapse of the First Republic, it managed, in 1993, to capture the largest of all northern cities, Milan, it has never since won elections there, its largest conquests instead coming in mid-ranking cities like Verona and Padua.

In Lega members' own accounts of why they joined the party, there is a strong promotion of both identity – the system of values that build a community – as well as the notion of being in contact with the population, where other parties have become more focused on media campaigns. In a Lega-sympathetic collection of testimony by Andrea Pannocchia and Susanna Ceccardi, one youth activist explains, 'The others look at us astonished because they don't have activism like this, by people active on the ground, holding gazebos, doing sit-ins, holding demonstrations and organising events';[19] or, as one activist put it, a 'school of life' running through activism.[20] A lawyer in Varese running a Lega-attached cultural association explains, 'It is a world of young people, professionals, entrepreneurs who perhaps don't want to dedicate themselves directly to politics but are interested in defending our territories' culture and environment'.[21] This is, indeed, a 'sense of community . . . not only as an administrative entity but something also spiritual, a territory where the human person rediscovers his own natural dimension and returns to relations based on affect rather than interest'.[22] Padanian identity, Islamophobia and a sense of being a victimised minority strongly colour the militants' own sense of togetherness – the left is often held to be both absent from communities, yet also culturally dominant.

Beyond this self-mythology, the Lega Nord's activist base – rooted among small businessmen and independent professionals outside the biggest cities – certainly does have material interests.[23] This is expressed both in a call for low taxes and the retreat of the central state, and the demand for its own heartland regions to keep more of their own tax revenues. In this sense, the Lega Nord put a special northern spin on the broader privatising and tax-cutting agenda advanced by the Pole of Freedoms coalition in the 1994 general election. This campaign, mounted together with Silvio Berlusconi, combined a classic neoliberal mix of the call to slim down what sociologist Pierre Bourdieu labelled the 'left hand' of the state – welfare, investment, public services – while also reinforcing its 'right hand', from law and order to subsidies for certain protected categories of business. This Pole of Freedoms alliance, standing in northern regions, stood separately from the so-called Pole of Good Government which Berlusconi sealed with the postfascist AN. Yet there were deep similarities, too: in each case an identitarian anti-communism was combined with a general offensive against *partitocrazia* and a confected 'outsiderishness'.

The ability of this outwardly populist and anti-political agenda to extend beyond parochial identitarianism was most strikingly illustrated by the alliances the Lega built. This was first notable in the curious trajectory of Emma Bonino, in 1994 a supporter of the Pole of Freedoms. A well-known liberal, she in fact spent most of her political career in the secularist Partito Radicale, fighting for such causes as abortion and divorce rights and the legalisation of cannabis. Such were her centrist credentials that in 2006–8 she became foreign minister in an administration led by the Democratic Party, and in 2018 leader of the small European-federalist party +Europa. Yet back in 1994 Bonino instead stood as an independent on a Lega Nord list, as part of the broader right-wing alliance. This was something of an eccentric choice but also had a clear logic, explained by Bonino in an interview with *Il Messaggero* in the run-up to the election. She emphasised that, while she had strong differences of political identity with the hard-right party, her liberal, free-market politics shared much in common with the Lega Nord's own call for a slimming of the Italian state:

> Many things divide us from the Lega, but it's also true that other things unite us, starting with [support for the] first-past-the-post electoral system. It's no accident that [she and fellow Radicals] successfully promoted, together with the Lega, the campaign for thirteen anti-statist and anti-corporatist referendums ... the vast majority of those who define themselves as progressives in reality embody a force for the conservation of the *partitocrazia* ... [We and the Lega are united] by the common battle against the *partitocrazia* and the wasting of public funds.

In the generally volatile situation of the early 1990s, liberals and *leghisti* united in the name of a Thatcherite revolution in Italy. As Bonino mentioned, this included a series of referendums cosponsored by the Lega Nord and her own Radicali, from privatising public broadcaster RAI to banning trade unions from directly collecting dues from workers' wages. Yet, if the campaign to finish off the First Republic was driven by actors spanning left–right divides, the alliances that emerged in 1994 were also liable to sudden and radical shifts. While upon its election Berlusconi's coalition enjoyed a large majority in the Chamber of Deputies, it would not even last one year in government. Relations were soon strained by revelations of the tycoon's collusion with the Sicilian Mafia and Calabrian 'Ndranghetà. Indeed, when news emerged that the media magnate faced fresh police investigations over his tax affairs, Bossi moved to split the coalition. But there was also a more strictly political reason behind the split: Berlusconi's public repudiation of the Lega Nord's plan to give the regions greater autonomy.

Bossi claimed that, in blocking this federalisation policy, concretised by the Lega Nord congress in November 1994, Berlusconi had reneged on his pre-election commitments to his allies. Yet in his bid to displace the tycoon's administration, Bossi also operated a radical shift of his own – allying with figures equally opposed to his northern-autonomist agenda. His close collaborator here was PCI veteran Massimo d'Alema, a leading figure in the PDS, able to promise the centre-left's votes for an alternative government. The two men's meeting at Bossi's little-used Rome address would rather bathetically be named the 'pact of the sardines' – an allusion to the sparse snacks that the Lega Nord leader was able to muster for his guests. It was nonetheless significant, as Bossi agreed to pull his party out of the Pole of Freedoms and join the PDS in backing an alternative administration led by former Bank of Italy director-general Lamberto Dini. This 'technical' government was appointed by president Eugenio Oscar Luigi Scalfaro in the name of piloting Italy toward a fresh general election, but it also had the task of 'cleaning up the public finances' – above all through a reform to cut the state's pension bill.

Supporters of this deal to back Dini characterised it as a break in 'political government', instead inaugurating an administration which could impose reforms that stood above ordinary party divides. Such an arrangement had been premiered in April 1993, in the final months of the First Republic, when former Bank of Italy governor Carlo Azeglio Ciampi was appointed head of a majority-DC cabinet, in the first republican administration to be led by an unelected figure. In the Italian political system, no prime minister is directly elected, and indeed it was only through the rise of Berlusconi (and later Renzi) that this office assumed such a strong electoral-media role, more akin to a presidential system. But what was new in the technical cabinets headed by first Ciampi then Dini was that they each relied on personnel drawn from outside the electoral arena, lifted to office in the name of correcting the inefficiencies of democratic politics. Every minister in Dini's cabinet was an unelected technocrat, and its base in parliament bore no reference to the coalitions that had stood in the 1994 general election.

The Dini government was also notable for enshrining a characteristic trait of the Second Republic, itself driven by Italy's changed international position. This cabinet of technocrats was built on the consensus that decisions were needed to adapt the Italian public finances to the conditions of the European Economic and Monetary Union, even if no democratically elected party wanted to take direct responsibility for implementing them. For the hard-right Lega as for the ex-Communist PDS, the pursuit of certain policies – and in particular the need for so-called 'balanced budgets', with rock-bottom levels of public borrowing – now stood above normal democratic competition. Even Forza Italia abstained on confidence votes during the Dini administration, rather than try to block its work. In the period of the post-2008 economic crisis, these principles would again assert themselves in the technocratic cabinet led by former

Goldman Sachs advisor Mario Monti from 2011 to 2013, as well as by the grand coalition that immediately followed it.

There was nothing incompatible between this logic and the Lega's identitarian radicalism, which in fact hardened in the period of its break with Berlusconi. Within just years of its founding, the Lega Nord had become a key force in a national government, throwing its weight behind a tycoon and then a former central banker in order to further its aim of trimming the Italian state. But the parliamentary pact with the PDS had not amounted to a wholesale dissolution of left-right divides. When the early general election came in April 1996 the Lega Nord found itself standing outside of both the main electoral blocs – and the results were para-doxical. While the Lega's overall vote share rose two points – to over 10 per cent of the national electorate – it was squeezed by the same first-past-the-post system that had powered its initial rise. Already in January 1995, Bossi's 'pact of the sardines' had seen his party lose 40 of its 118 MPs, who remained loyal to Berlusconi's Pole of Freedoms. With the 1996 general election, the Lega was reduced to just 59 seats in the Chamber of Deputies.

The Lega's attempt to deal with these setbacks was defined less by a move to the right as by the sharper stance it now adopted against the central Italian state. Having repudiated the centre-right alliance and Berlusconi, Bossi pushed for a change in the party's image, adopting an openly secessionist agenda. As the promise of reforming the Italian state waned, in 1997 Bossi renamed the party the 'Lega Nord for the Independence of Padania', insisting that this 'country' strad-dling the Po Valley from the Alps to the Adriatic should cast off the South altogether. Yet, if this secessionism marked a sharp break from the typical codes of republican politics, there were also elements of continuity with the agenda the Lega Nord had followed in backing Dini. With Italy widely expected to fail to meet the convergence criteria to join the euro upon its launch in 1999, Bossi insisted that the wealthier northern regions should not allow the South to drag them down: a new and independent Padania would, instead, be able to take its place in the concert of European nations.

There were certain tensions between the Lega Nord's pro-business agenda and its folk nationalism – the radical-right party's secessionism represented a clear destabilising force in Italian politics. Yet Bossi also sought to diversify the party's image and make it more like the 'nation' it sought to rally. This was the impetus behind the unofficial Padanian Parliament it created in 1997, which would supposedly serve as the launchpad for a new state. In this cause, a series of Potemkin parties were organised, from the Padanian Communists (whose candidates included one M. Salvini), to a list aligned to Bonino's Radicals, or the top-placed lists, respectively named European Democrats – Padanian Labour and Liberal Democrats. The Lega claimed that around six million people had participated in this vote – far beyond its own four million tally in the 1996 general election. The institution created by this election had no actual powers. Yet this also set a precedent by which the Lega Nord used unofficial referendums to mobilise its own base, a dress rehearsal designed to show that a Padanian state could, or even would, soon come into being.

In Government, against Rome

Yet Padanian secessionism brought major strategic problems, even in elections for regional councils – bodies with a wide array of powers over health care, education and transport, as well as an important platform for propaganda. And the Lega had no chance of securing absolute majorities in such councils without the aid of the wider, all-Italian centre-right parties. In the 1996 general election, the party had been isolated from both main political blocs, and the success of Romano Prodi's centre-left government in bringing Italy into the euro in 1999 scotched even the notional possibility of Padania joining the single currency on its own. Bossi's politics of slimming down the state and pushing privatisation were now the mainstream, but its pro-independence stance was minoritarian. It was thus caught between its ability to mobilise a radical minority, including in party activism, and its need to form broader alliances to win first-past-the-post contests. Hence, for all its rhetoric on the impossibility of reforming the Italian state, by the 1999 European elections the Lega Nord had turned back toward a pact with Forza Italia and the smaller right-wing parties. Just as the experience of 1994–96 had highlighted Berlusconi's need to keep the Lega on the side, Bossi would, over the next two decades, repeatedly return to electoral pacts with his eternal brother enemy.

In the era bracketed by the war on terror and the financial crisis, the Lega Nord's involvement in the Berlusconi governments of 2001–6 and 2008–11 would begin its conversion into a more conventionally hard-right force, indeed the tycoon's strongest ally within the centre-right coalition. Even beyond the Bossi-Berlusconi connection, there were also specific areas of accord between the postfascists and the Lega. Having at least muted its commitment to destroy the Italian state, around the turn of the millennium, the northern chauvinist party increasingly took up the campaign against immigration. In 2001, Bossi buried the hatchet with AN's Gianfranco Fini to co-author a bill that massively expanded the apparatus of migrant detention and expulsion. At the same time, in the bid to maintain an ersatz 'outsiderishness', Bossi increasingly resorted to shock communication tactics, for instance in his comments that the navy ought to fire on the boats of arriving refugees. This harsh identitarianism – expressed in the form of victimhood – was also put on display in election posters portraying a Native American with the tagline 'They didn't control immigration, now they live on reserves!'

The Lega Nord's tonal divergence from the codes of republican institutions sat oddly with its actual presence in government. Clinging to their own territorial identity, Bossi's activist base did not warm to Berlusconi or even to *leghista* officials serving in 'the Rome government' like interior minister Roberto Maroni. They could, at least, content themselves with the idea that the party represented a regionalist opposition *within* government ranks. This balancing of 'Padanian' and Italian commitments was most theatrically demonstrated by the Lega's Luca Zaia, agriculture minister from 2008 to 2010, who led protests outside his own ministry in order to demand more funds for his home region. His insistence on more cash for wealthy Veneto would have made little sense for a genuinely national politician. Yet such bizarre antics also suited the *leghista* minister's plans for what came next, serving as a kind of foreplay for his campaign to become president of this region. While the Lega Nord had no chance of securing regional government if it stood outside the centre-right alliance, the pact with Berlusconi allowed it to take Veneto for the first time in 2010, as well as the Piedmont region surrounding Turin.

Compared to the Forza Italia ministers chosen from among Berlusconi's personal associates, Zaia and his colleagues were far more bound by the politics of their home regions as well as their accountability to party activists. This owed not only to the Lega's regionalist identity but also the fact that its organisation was based on a mass of territorial branches. This accountability to local cadres – whose sources of funds and institutional weight also rose with break-throughs in regional and mayoral elections – contrasted with the 'light' organisational form pioneered by Berlusconi, in which posts and influence remained under the tight control of the party's owner-proprietor. Even amid the general volatility of the Second Republic, in which campaign vehicles like Forza Italia did away with 'dense' mass-party structures, Bossi's Lega Nord was built on an organisational model more akin to its 1980s counterparts, sometimes even called a 'Leninist' model. Rallied in a force that had arisen in opposition to the First Republic, the *leghisti* nonetheless carried forth some of the assumptions of the previous era of political engagement. Indeed, already by the time of the 1996 general election the Lega Nord was the oldest party represented in the Italian Parliament.

If the 1990s saw widespread claims in the death of the mass-party form – exemplified by the wider collapse of the First Republic – the Lega Nord's history instead highlights the merits of this more rooted model, allowing the party to endure even severe defeats. Its mass membership – hitting 112,000 by 1992 – was an impressive countertendency, especially considering that one could not simply sign up as a member of the Lega; rather, one had to earn membership through activism and attendance at meetings. This deep sense of ongoing party commitment, combined with the regionalist identity of which the Lega boasted under Bossi's leadership, made it quite unlike the media machines with which it clashed each election time. As recent research on Lega membership structures has highlighted,[24] its territorial roots are maintained not only through such practices as party gazebos (a way of maintaining direct contact with local populations) but also regular member meetings with elected officials as well as parallel and voluntary organisations representing such groups as women and youth.

As we shall see further on, today's Lega is less rooted in local branches, or indeed 'Padanian' identity, than it was under Bossi's leadership. From 2011, not long before Bossi was forced from office, to Salvini's electoral breakthrough in 2018, the party's number of territorial sections in fact fell by over two-thirds, from 1,451 to 437.[25] Yet, through the volatile times of the Second Republic, these deeper structures had rendered the Lega Nord far hardier than its rivals, time and again proving able to renew itself notwithstanding the electoral setbacks that followed each spell in government. The party had not just ridden the ideological wave of 'Bribesville', with its revolt against the corrupt party system in Rome, but also, paradoxically, created a vehicle much more similar to the mass parties that Clean Hands had destroyed. This laid both the political and organisational bases for the Lega's conquest of small towns across northern Italy, a bedrock that survived even Bossi's own downfall.

The Revolution Eats Its Children

As we have seen, Bossi's leadership of the Lega Nord was shaped by the tension between its regionalist and national ambitions. Throughout his period of control, and especially after the party's first spell in national office in 1994, Bossi sought to present himself as a 'guarantor' figure, who would protect the interests of members against any corrupting effect that serving in the Rome government might have on ministers. The rise of a layer of *leghista* ministers, MPs, and European and regional/local representatives created what some activists derided as 'the party of the blue cars', supposedly focused on maintaining their own perks. From the very top of the organisational machine, Bossi could, in part at least, sidestep such an accusation. His only ministerial role in Berlusconi's governments ('Minister for Devolution') was a purely propagandistic one, allowing him to keep one foot outside of the central Italian state and claim to represent the *leghista* base directly rather than the government as a whole. As his election posters put it: 'further from Rome, closer to you'.

Whereas the Lega's anti-corruption stance had soon brought Berlusconi's first government to retreat and then collapse,[26] the alliances of the 2000s were more governed by a tacit division of control. Here, Bossi's party was allowed to lead the broader centre-right alliance in its heartlands in exchange for backing national-level legislation that shielded Berlusconi's interests. Where, in 1994, the Lega had withdrawn its backing for the Biondi bill in the face of public pressure, over Berlusconi's subsequent spells in office (2001–6 and then 2008–11), it instead gave its support to the billionaire tycoon's *ad personam* legislation. This included backing for the infamous Gasparri bill, which protected Berlusconi's media empire, or the measures known as Lodo Schifani and Lodo Alfano, to protect ministers from police investigation. When the Constitutional Court threatened to block this latter bill, Bossi said he was prepared to 'lead the people in arms' to 'defend democracy'.[27]

The contradictions in the Lega's anti-corruption agenda were not limited to its ties to Berlusconi – rather, they were also reflected in its own internal structures. Already in the Clean Hands years, Bossi had appeared in a dual guise, cheering on the magistrates before being called into the dock himself. But, while Bossi's admission of illicit funding from the Montedison industrial group had seen him escape with a suspended sentence – sparing the Lega any immediate political fall out – his own opaque control made party funds increasingly inscrutable. When Bossi suffered a stroke in 2004 (forcing him to miss the Pontida rally, which was, in turn, cancelled), he opted not to begin a succession process, but rather to centralise his authority against potential rivals for the leadership. The 'magic circle' of party insiders organised by his wife excluded even figures like Interior Minister Maroni and began treating the party as well as its finances like family property. Though Bossi purported to play an executive role in the Lega, allowing him to discipline the ministers in Rome, in fact he was unaccountable to the base.

The end of Berlusconi's last government in autumn 2011, which again pushed the Lega into opposition, was soon followed by the final explosion of this set-up. On 8 January 2012, *Il Secolo XIX* newspaper broke the news that Lega Nord treasurer Francesco Belsito, a Bossi appointee, had illicitly drawn on state funds from Cyprus and Tanzania, using the cash to provide personal favours to fellow members of the 'magic circle'. Three days later, the scandal intensified as Bossi voted to shield from prosecution Nicola Cosentino, an MP from Berlusconi's party who had been arrested for his alleged ties to the Naples mafia. The combination of internal impropriety and support for Berlusconi finally provoked a revolt in the *leghista* base, who called on Maroni to take action to reclaim the party. Bossi went on the counteroffensive, cancelling all public meetings involving the former interior minister. Nine days later, a protest against Mario Monti's centrist government instead became the scene of an open clash between followers of these rival Lega leaders.

Revelations into the Lega's dubious financial practices followed thick and fast, highlighting the webs of corruption and ties to organised crime that had built up under Bossi's leadership. Indeed, it was a case starkly reminiscent of those that had felled the parties of the First Republic. The regional government in Lombardy – a key *leghista* heartland – itself came under investigation for ties to 'Ndrangheta, the Calabrian Mafia, and by early April, the leadership crisis had become unmanageable. As the prosecutors closed in, Bossi was forced to abandon the role he had held for over two decades. Amid a string of resignations, Maroni became new party secretary, promising a clean-up operation in Lega Nord ranks as well as a bid to assume the same powers that Bossi had enjoyed, maintaining its hierarchical structure. Yet it was a young cadre in the affections of both men – Matteo Salvini – who took over the leadership of the Lega Lombarda, vowing to shake off the figures who had dragged its name through the mud.

This was not the end of the Lega Nord's crisis – indeed, in the February 2013 general election, it hit a fresh low. Even faced with Mario Monti's unpopular technocratic government, supported by both the Democrats and Forza Italia, the Lega was unable to turn attention away from its own internal woes. Having lost two-thirds of its members since 2010, the Lega Nord took just 4.3 per cent of the vote, or half its 2008 score. This was, in political terms, a historic nadir. Back in 2001, the Lega Nord had shed even more votes after its series of U-turns on the independence question. Yet then it had been saved by the wider context of right-wing advance, allowing it again to play a kingmaker role in forming the subsequent centre-right government. The 2013 defeat offered no such consolation, as the Lega slumped into near-irrelevance while the M5S soared to first place. The message that 'the politicians in Rome' were all the same was now being championed by a newer force – and directed against the Lega itself.

Two decades after the corrupt PSI man Mario Chiesa's bid to flush his payload, the forces that had broken up the First Republic were being eaten by their own revolution. The accusations even struck at Antonio di Pietro, the protagonist of Clean Hands and leader of the small centre-left party Italia dei Valori (Italy of Values; IdV). On 28 October 2012, he was targeted by RAI's *Report*, an investigative current affairs programme that emerged during the wave of judicial populism. Di Pietro was accused of keeping €50 million of electoral expenses under own family's control, while building up a real-estate empire supposedly including fifty-six properties. Faced with scandalised editorials, Di Pietro strongly denied the allegations of impropriety and even brought a successful libel action against the producers. But, as he put it immediately after the accusations were aired, IdV had 'died on Sunday night's *Report*'. The new era in Italian public life had personalised everything – and for someone who claimed to stand only for anti-corruption, it was political death to see one's claim to clean hands tarnished.

IdV was, indeed, destroyed: even after removing Di Pietro, it lost all its seats in the February 2013 general election. The setbacks for the Lega Nord were not quite so bad, for it did at least retain its northern fortresses – thus surviving the departure of its own founder-leader. Following the election, Bossi's successor Maroni departed the front line of national politics to focus on his role as president of the Lombardy region. With the *leghisti* now able to count on only one in twenty-five voters nationally, the contest to succeed him might have looked like rather a footnote. Yet Matteo Salvini's victory in the internal ballot – thumping the disgraced Bossi by more than a four-to-one margin – would prove decisive amid the turmoil that followed. In August 2013, Berlusconi was finally sentenced for a fraud conviction, with no further recourse to appeal. Where the Lega founder had burned out his political capital, the billionaire tycoon was formally banned from holding public office. Rising to the Lega leadership as the men who built the Second Republic reached their downfall, Salvini promised a further revolution on the right – one fit for a new age in Italian politics.

2

'Say Something Left-wing!'

The weakened ties between voters, parties, and institutions aren't just an Italian phenomenon. Political scientists such as Peter Mair have spoken of the historic decline of mass parties across the West in recent decades.[1] Arising around the turn of the twentieth century, these parties based themselves on local associational activity and an engaged community of militants, in contrast to the elite parliamentary factions more typical of the nineteenth century. Yet their 'dense' democratic structures, bound to the day-to-day activism of their cadres and mass membership, have increasingly given way to technocratic 'cartel parties', which base their power on their control of institutional resources and professionalised marketing operations. This has driven the process known as Pasokification, in which parties which allow their social roots to wither over decades then fall victim to abrupt electoral wipeouts. The phenomenon is named after Greece's PASOK, whose role in a series of austerity and grand-coalition governments saw its support collapse from 44 per cent in 2009 to under 5 per cent in 2015; in the crisis period its malaise has also spread to historic parties like France's Parti Socialiste and, somewhat more gradually, Germany's Social Democratic Party. Yet, already in the early 1990s, the fall of Italy's First Republic provided a test run of what politics looks like when mass parties are removed from the scene.

The result in the Italian 'laboratory' has not been to create other, stable parties in place of the old, but rather to feed an ever-exasperated climate of volatility, as even residual and inherited political identities crumble. Popular detachment from established parties or anger at self-serving elites does not necessarily lead to positive outcomes in terms of democratic engagement. Such sentiments may both draw on and radicalise a mood of despair and impotence, or they may feed the sense that since all politicians are thieves there is no choice to be had between them, and thus no point participating in the democratic process. In the Italian case, the conviction that politics can do nothing for ordinary citizens has, in fact, fed a historic rise in voter abstention. While the polarised general election campaigns of the 1970s, at the height of Enrico Berlinguer's Partito Comunista Italiano (Italian Communist Party; PCI), saw turnouts of well over 90 per cent, today this figure has fallen by almost a third. The lawfare that felled the First Republic created not more accountability, but an increasingly personalised and volatile political field. As former magistrate Antonio di Pietro acknowledged in 2017, after the demise of his Italy of Values party, 'Clean Hands produced a void, from which began personalised parties, starting with me. But they are parties that last the space of a morning – something of which I am the living proof'.

The destruction of mass parties – and the associated rise of political 'stars' with their base in media and the entertainment industry – has drastically reduced the spaces of popular representation. The Italians who have lost the most economically over the last three decades look a lot like those who used to vote for left-wing parties – the so-called popular classes, a category encompassing such groups as blue- and white-collar workers, small traders, and the unemployed. These groups have, since the 1990s, experienced a historic fall in their living standards, bearing the brunt of austerity and falling public investment as the economy flatlines. But not only have they lost their ties to the institutional left, they are in general less politically active. As we saw in Chapter 1, territorially rooted parties did not depart the scene entirely. Despite its leader-focused model, which managed even to survive the departure of its original boss, the Lega is a fine example of the power of activist politics rooted in territorial structures. But the popular classes today lack any distinct forms of representation; they are no longer gathered in party or trade union structures or even mobilised around shared economic interests. As we shall see, not only have their old parties disappeared, but their whole terrain of political action has been impoverished.

The sense that the "people of the left" have lost their political voice is most famously symbolised by a scene in *Aprile*, a 1998 comedy film directed by and starring Nanni Moretti. Like much of the popular director's work, *Aprile* provides an ironic take on Moretti's own position as a former Communist deprived of his political home, in an age of rising Berlusconism. The film's most iconic scene centres on a televised debate from the 1994 general election, in which the billionaire tycoon is confronted by Partito Democratico della

Sinistra (Democratic Party of the Left; PDS) leader Massimo D'Alema. Or rather, not confronted. For as Berlusconi rants against the supposed 'Communist' magistrates, D'Alema sits in passive silence, prompting Moretti's character to shout at his TV: 'Say something left-wing! Anything! Even say something that isn't left-wing, just a bit of civility!'

Ironically, this quote would enter the collective memory clipped to just the first four words – as an indictment of those who had entered politics as Communists but then rebranded themselves as anything but. D'Alema epitomised this phenomenon – he is mockingly nicknamed *El Líder Máximo* for his mix of abrasive arrogance, veneration of historic PCI leader Palmiro Togliatti, and bid to cast himself as a moderate centrist. Indeed, when his PDS did finally enter government in 1996, together with its centre-left allies, this was hardly the triumph of the PCI's bid to change the republic's institutions from within. It instead set a precedent by which the centre-left recast itself as a force for the neoliberal modernisation of Italy, moreover representing competence and sobriety as against the dangers of the populist right. Indeed, Moretti's call for a focus on 'civility' would become common sense – but 'saying something left-wing' would not. The PDS and its successors were, instead, decisive in the mass-scale privatisation of public assets and the stripping-away of labour rights inherited from the First Republic, even while it painted itself in the watercolours of progressivism through its embrace of Europeanism and a smattering of civil rights measures. After he became premier in late 1998, D'Alema however went even further in the repudiation of the Communist past, joining the NATO offensive against Yugoslavia in the name of humanitarian intervention.

Table 2.1. THE DOUBLE COLLAPSE OF THE LEFT-WING ELECTORATE
General election results for left-wing and centre-left parties, 1979–2018

Year	Votes by party			
				Total
1979	11,139,231 (PCI)	3,630,052 (PSI)	796,709 (Others)	15,566,052
1983	11,032,318 (PCI)	4,223,362 (PSI)	542,039 (DP)	15,797,791
1987	10,250,644 (PCI)	5,501,696 (PSI)	641,901 (DP)	16,394,241
1992	6,321,084 (PDS)	5,343,930 (PSI)	2,204,641 (PRC)	13,869,655
1994	7,881,646 (PDS)	2,343,946 (PRC)	849,429 (PSI)	11,075,021
1996	7,894,118 (PDS)		3,213,748 (PRC)	11,107,866
2001	6,151,154 (DS)	1,868,659 (PRC)	620,859 (PdCI)	8,640,672
2006	11,930,983 (UU)	2,229,464 (PRC)	884,127 (PdCI)	15,044,574
2008	12,095,306 (PD)	1,124,298 (La Sinistra—Arcobaleno)		13,219,604
2013	8,646,034 (PD)	1,089,231 (SEL)	765,189 (RC)	10,500,454
2018	6,161,896 (PD)	1,114,799 (LeU)	372,179 (PaP)	7,648,874

Note. PCI = Partito Comunista Italiano (Italian Communist Party); PSI = Partito Socialista Italiano (Italian Socialist Party); DP = Democrazia Proletaria (Proletarian Democracy); PDS = Partito Democratico della Sinistra (Democratic Party of the Left); PRC = Partito della Rifondazione Comunista (Communist Refoundation Party); PdCI = Partito dei Comunisti Italiani (Party of Italian Communists); PD = Partito Democratic (Democratic Party); SEL = Sinistra Ecologia Libertà (Left Ecology Freedom) ; RC = Rivoluzione Civile (Civic Revolution); LeU = Liberi e Uguali (Free and Equal); PaP = Potere al Popolo (Power to the People).
Source: Interior Ministry data.

The break with the PCI took place under the banner of renewal – in laying rest to the Communist name in 1991, the PDS's leaders claimed to be continuing the mother party's own previous turn away from the Soviet model and toward the 'European socialism' embodied by forces like the German SPD, blending social democracy with liberal pro-Europeanism. This was also bound up with a certain vision of the death of class politics, according to which rising white-collar layers identified less with collective or material interests than the PCI's old industrial heartlands, and instead sought representation of their progressive cultural values. Yet, while its former base had certainly fragmented, the subjective choices of PDS leaders reified this shift, leaping toward something less like the reformist wing of the labour movement and more akin to US liberalism. For too long, the PCI had toiled under the pall of a socialist end goal that its leaders never expected to achieve; now, with the collapse of its historic rivals, they could finally mount a wholesale change of political identity. With Berlusconi and his far-right allies serving as the ideal enemy to unite against, former PCI members joined with the centrist orphans of Christian Democracy in a new centre-left bloc.

The PCI and PSI were the main forces of the labour movement in the First Republic. The PCI turned into the PDS in 1991 with some factions splitting to form the Partito della Rifondazione Comunista (Communist Refoundation Party; PRC), in turn becoming DS in 1998, while the PSI collapsed over 1992–93 caused by revelations of its deep involvement in Bribesville. Other parties mentioned in Table 2.1 include the far-left Democrazia Proletaria (DP), which joined PRC, and the Partito dei Comunisti Italiani (PdCI), a group that formed after a 1998 split in the PRC.

Table 2.2 SOCIO-PROFESSIONAL DISTRIBUTION
OF VOTE, 2018 (MAIN PARTIES)

Socio-professional distribution of voters (per cent)	Political party (percentage of vote for Chamber of Deputies)					
	Liberi e Uguali (3 per cent)	Democrats + allies (23 per cent)	Forza Italia (14 per cent)	Lega (Nord) (17 per cent)	Fratelli d'Italia (4 per cent)	Movimento 5 Stelle (33 per cent)
Unemployed	3	11	14	12	1	57
Blue-collar	3	10	12	20	2	43
Students	5	24	12	15	2	36
Pensioners	2	40	18	15	6	38
Trader/small-business/artisan	2	13	13	29	2	35
Housewives	2	13	19	24	5	35
Self-employed professional	5	22	11	15	4	27
Technical/white-collar/managerial	5	22	10	16	7	33
Other	2	16	12	13	1	43

Source: Adapted from Ilvo Diamanti et al., *Divergenze parallele*, Bari: Laterza, 2018.

The development of a new centre-left alliance was encouraged by the majoritarian electoral law introduced in 1993, which was designed to create a binary system of centre-left and centre-right forces on the US model. The PDS strongly backed this move, which also undermined the viability of forces to its left, which were instead continually blackmailed into backing the centre-left for fear that dividing the vote would aid Berlusconi. In the 1996 general election, the centre-left l'Ulivo coalition led by former DC man Romano Prodi came in first place, with 42 per cent of the vote for the Chamber of Deputies: its largest single element was the PDS (21 per cent), representing half of the centre-left's total score. The PDS did not represent a distinctive left-wing pole within l'Ulivo, but rather used this coalition as its own path toward a more openly free-market agenda, as an agent of economic 'liberalisation' unbound from its former base. In this vein, the Party of the Democratic Left became the Democrats of the Left (DS). In 2006, the DS was part of the Uniti nell'Ulivo (UU) list together with Christian Democrats and liberals; the following year these forces together formed a Democratic Party (PD), openly inspired by the Clintonite wing of the Democratic Party in the United States.

This liberal turn was, at the same time, a break with earlier mass-party models, which reached its apogee in the early 2010s under Matteo Renzi's hyperpersonalised leadership. Inheriting most of the PCI's hundreds of local offices, the PDS–DS–PD did retain more of the trappings of a party than forces like Forza Italia or M5S. Yet with the integration of liberal-centrist parliamentary factions, the role of mass-membership structures rooted in the labour movement was consistently marginalised. This was notable in the decision to import US-style primaries – not only prioritising person-ality over policy but also diminishing the value of regular membership as opposed to merely signing up as a supporter. This weakened attachment is also reflected in the bases of unity themselves: whereas the PCI had been cohered by tradition, shared material interest and at least a formal commitment to the socialist future, today's PD is instead, in essence, a party of the liberal middle classes existing for the purpose of electoral competition alone. Yet if this turn is easily misrepresented as an act of opportunism, the new model has brought a sharp fall in the left-wing electorate, as we see in Table 2.1. In its final decade, the PCI experienced a gradual loss of support, from 11.1 million votes in 1979 to 10.3 million in 1987. Yet the centre-left of subsequent years has suffered a much more drastic decline, neither holding on to the old PCI electorate nor replacing it with others.

Table 2.3 2018 DISTRIBUTION OF 1987 VOTERS for the PCI and DC

Party voted for in 1987	Voting distribution in 2018 elections	
	Abstentions	Party
PCI	20 per cent	M5S (35 per cent) PD (32 per cent) LeU (10 per cent) Lega (9 per cent) PaP (5 per cent) Others (5 per cent)
DC	32 per cent	Forza Italia (29 per cent) Lega (20 per cent) PD (18 per cent) M5S (18 per cent) Others (15 per cent)

Note. PCI = Partito Comunista Italiano (Italian Communist Party); M5S = Movimento Cinque Stelle (Five Star Movement); PD = Partito Democratic (Democratic Party); LeU = Liberi e Uguali (Free and Equal); PaP = Potere al Popolo (Power to the People); DC = Democrazia Cristiana (Christian Democracy). Source: SWG.

That party's historic base has, indeed, become extremely fragmented, with less than half of it still aligned to the centre-left and left-wing parties that resulted from the splits of 1991. Telling evidence of this came in a survey by pollster SWG after the March 2018 election, which surveyed Italians who had voted for the PCI in its last general election run back in 1987 (Table 2.3). Those who had voted in this contest were, by definition, at least forty-eight years old, placing them in age brackets generally more inclined to vote PD. Yet, in 2018, it was M5S that placed first among these ex-PCI voters, at 35 per cent, as against 32 per cent for the PD. This was consistent with studies that showed M5S's good scores among social categories among which the PCI had once enjoyed majority support – including some 57 per cent of the unemployed and 43 per cent of blue-collar voters (Table 2.2). The PD, conversely, came in first place only among pensioners – as a study by the Centro Italiano Studi Elettorali showed, its vote was directly proportional to class, in the sense that the *richer* the voter, the *likelier* they were to vote for the main party of the centre-left.[2] Parties to the left of the PD scored weakly, if rather better among ex-PCI voters. The social-democratic list led by figures like D'Alema and Bersani, Liberi e Uguali (Free and Equal), took just 3.4 per cent of the vote nationally, and Rifondazione and its allies in Potere al Popolo (Power to the People) 1.1 per cent; among 1987 PCI supporters they took 10 and 5 per cent, respectively; Matteo Salvini's Lega took 9 per cent.

If this survey casts doubt on the notion that the Lega is really conquering the former PCI's particular base of supporters, rather than mobilising previous right-wing or non-voters, the 2018 election did show how far the left has lost its own historic social referent. This bears some comparison to the Pasokification of social-democratic parties elsewhere in Europe, though nowhere else has the main centre-left force become so totally a party of the professional middle classes. If, in Spain, France, or Greece, the withering of such parties has given rise to alternative forces claiming to uphold their original spirit, Italy has instead seen a more general destruction of the left, in which the fragmented social categories it once rallied either turn to M5S or abstain. Three decades of economic woe, discredited institutions, and declining parties have undermined popular faith in political action – creating a scorched-earth situation in which the forces of the left are unable to articulate any positive vision of Italy's future. This is also storing up dangerous long-term effects. If the SWG survey suggested that elderly ex-PCI voters still retain some identitarian bind to the left, young Italians in dire economic straits seem unlikely to seek redemption through parties with no recent record of serving their material interests. Far from the focus of the centre-left, these social groups lost the most from its time in power.

The End of the PCI

The unravelling of popular mobilisation is closely bound up with the end of the PCI, which had since 1945 been the dominant political expression of Italian labour. Not only the effects of its collapse on activists' emotions and identity, but also the generational shifts that set it into its final crisis, were decisive here. A party that claimed to represent *il popolo* and not just the blue-collar *classe operaia*, the PCI attached its Marxist-inflected class vision of society to a broader popular interest, integrating the demands of white-collar employees, small-shop owners, and farmers. This also gave it a broad electoral base – indeed, after scoring 22.6 per cent in the 1953 general election,[3] its vote continually rose in national contests, to a peak of 34.4 per cent in 1976. However, already by 1980, the trade unions' defeats in red 'fortresses' like Turin's Mirafiori FIAT plant had called into question the PCI's vision of industrial modernity and the future centrality of blue-collar Italy to any broad class alliance. In this same period, the PCI was further undermined by the crisis of Eastern Bloc socialism and indeed a generational problem, as its cadres trained in the Resistance era finally began to retreat from the front line of politics. Facing eclipse by the Socialists and dismayed by the failure of reforms in the Soviet Union, in 1991 the PCI finally broke with its historic communist identity, turning into the PDS. Around one in ten members upheld the old banner, which was reconstituted as the PRC.

Already we have seen how the destruction of the First Republic coincided with a wider liberal triumphalism – the credo that the 'bloated' Italian state ought to be replaced by a slimmed down, rationalised, depoliticised administration, run on the model of a business. This shift in public discourse owed not only to the entrepreneur-premier Berlusconi, but also to forces on the left who had more recently embraced the values of liberal capitalism. While the centre-right literally put an entrepreneur and his business associates at the heart of public life, the centre-left of the Second Republic period instead supported a series of governments led by institutional figures and central bankers. This was a clear break with the left's historic mission. The Constitution written by the Resistance parties in the wake of World War II had not just invoked the supremacy of popular interests over private profit, but tied this to the democratisation of public life. Article 3 proclaims that 'It is the duty of the Republic to remove those obstacles of an economic or social nature which constrain the freedom and equality of citizens, thereby impeding the full development of the human person and the effective participation of all workers in the political, economic and social organisation of the country'. This was anything but the centre-left's focus in the 1990s. Former Communists instead allied with the champions of deregulation and neoliberal economics, even to the point of entrenching fiscal austerity into the Constitution itself.

As Stathis Kouvelakis wrote in an article on the political nihilism of former left-wingers, the fulsome praise for the key institutions of Western capitalism coming from former PCI leader Achille Occhetto – declaring Wall Street the 'temple of civilisation' – would have been hard to imagine from any ordinary social democrat.[4] This, instead, rather more fitted the needs of a former Communist who sought a quick means of reinventing himself. Yet just as the Lega made inroads into Christian Democracy even in the latter stages of the First Republic era, it should be recognised that the hollowing out of the PCI had begun long before the party's formal demise, with the failure of Enrico Berlinguer's project to draw the party into a reformist coalition. Where in the mid-1970s Berlinguer had promised to overcome the divide between the labour movement and the institutions of the republic by bringing the PCI into concert with the Christian Democrats, this represented a significant narrowing of the party's transformative horizons, which moreover entailed an immediate 'policy of sacrifices' for its working-class base. In postwar decades, the PCI had posed itself as a modernising alternative to the DC. Yet by the turn of the 1980s its project was at a dead end, as it proved neither able to take over national institutions or build a further oppositional base in its industrial heartlands.

Having become a truly mass party at the end of World War II, the PCI had been renowned across the western European Left for its bid to extend beyond a blue-collar electorate, embracing a wider popular interest. This latter was rallied by the PCI's diverse forms of mobilisation both within and beyond the workplace context as – in obedience to Palmiro Togliatti's vision of Gramscianism – the party sought to spread its influence at all levels of social and public life. Unable to enter government at the national level because of the Cold War *conventio ad excludendum*, the PCI nonetheless built its own counter-institutions within the First Republic, including a vast apparatus of party-attached consumer and worker cooperatives, integrating up to 8 million Italians. The creation of regional governments in 1970 as well as the PCI's advance in local politics moreover allowed it to advance an Italian version of municipal socialism, most famously developed in 'Red Bologna'.[5] Retaining a specifically communist rather than social-democratic identity, the PCI married a vague future promise of socialism with the community built around the party and the reforms achieved in the present, from free public transport to the generous payments for industrial workers made redundant.

The PCI's identity was, however, far from simply antagonistic or anti-capitalist. Indeed, it married this social rootedness with a certain sense of moral superiority over the Christian Democrats and Socialists – a claim strengthened by its exclusion from national government. Italy was, indeed, one of few European countries where the main party of labour was never integrated into national office. Backed by up to one-third of Italians, the PCI especially identified with the Constitution written by the Resistance parties after World War II, calling for the full realisation of its democratic promise. This sense of historic mission was famously expressed in Pier Paolo Pasolini's 1974 *Corriere della Sera* article 'I know', which exalted the PCI as 'the saving grace of Italy and its meagre democratic institutions'.[6] The poet and filmmaker described the party as 'a clean country in a dirty country, an honest country in a dishonest country, an intelligent country in an idiotic country, an educated country in an ignorant country, a humanist country in a consumerist country'.[7] Himself a dissident PCI supporter, ostracised on account of his homosexuality, Pasolini nonetheless richly rendered its self-image as an island of the future that needed to establish 'diplomatic relations' with the other Italy – almost like another country divided by the Cold War.

The PCI had, since 1945, championed a vision of growth based on the community of producer interests, in the immediate postwar months even forcing through wage cuts in the higher interests of reconstruction. This idea was powerfully invoked by the 1947 Constitution, which described Italy as a 'democratic republic founded on labour.' Yet, even amidst the sustained 'economic miracle' of the 1950s and 1960s – in which Italian growth rates outpaced all European countries except West Germany – Italy lacked the corporatist structures that might have allowed a true pact between labour and capital. The wage gains and employment protections won in this period instead came through powerful shop floor movements or, more indirectly, through the reforms achieved by socialists in DC-led governments. Yet amidst mounting social conflict in the 1970s, the PCI's Enrico Berlinguer proposed a 'historic compromise' to 'unblock' Italian democracy, from 1976 offering external support to Giulio Andreotti's DC government in the name of 'national solidarity'. The PCI's lack of a direct say (or ministers, for that matter) in the DC cabinet radicalised its prior tendency to see labour as a stakeholder in the national interest rather than in terms of a direct offensive against capital.

After the death of its historic leader Togliatti in 1964, the PCI would remain divided between different visions of Italian economic development, as represented on the left by Pietro Ingrao and on the right by Giorgio Amendola and Giorgio Napolitano. Whereas Ingrao emphasised the need to break out of a low-wage model and promote demand-led growth, in an age of both rising consumer society and the integration of the Socialists into high office, the *amendoliani* instead held to more liberal ideas focused on the need to complete the bourgeois-democratic revolution in a 'backward' Italy. Enrico Berlinguer's election as general secretary at the PCI's 1972 Congress looked like a defeat for Amendola's more liberal *migliorista* faction, yet, under his leadership, the party would move significantly to the right both in its stance toward the DC and its economic outlook. Over subsequent years, its answer to slowing growth and rising inflation was anything but distinctively 'communist' and was increasingly characterised by a critique of a bloated state machine. By the end of the 1970s, as it sought a 'historic compromise' with the DC in an era of mounting recession, the PCI began to uphold ideas of the same stamp being pushed internationally by the rising neoliberals.

In the 1976 general election the PCI came closer than ever to a historic *sorpasso* (overtake) of the DC – as it scored a record 34.4 per cent of the vote – and immediately angled toward government. In a bid to show its institutional responsibility it allowed the DC to govern alone, first through abstaining in confidence votes, then in actively voting for Andreotti's cabinet, despite having no ministers of its own. As with any turn mounted by the PCI, the party also rationalised this theoretically – including its support for Andreotti's austerity measures. Its new approach was especially informed by the ideas of Italian-American economist Franco Modigliani, at the Massachusetts Institute of Technology. Though initially known as a Keynesian, Modigliani had become a leading defender of a quite different set of ideas, which focused on suppressing inflation by both restraining wage demands and preventing the unemployment level from sinking too low (as encapsulated in his noninflationary rate of unemployment hypothesis, later known as nonaccelerating-inflation rate of unemployment, NAIRU).[8] As Francesco Cattabrini writes in a fascinating study, the PCI's embrace of Modigliani's ideas in effect meant abandoning the call to keep wages aligned to price increases, instead allowing them to fall in the overall interests of economic growth.[9] These theoretical postulates, embraced by a 1976 conference of the PCI-linked Centro Studi sulle Politiche Economiche attended by Modigliani, suggested that the party should support austerity in the name of aiding Italy's international competitiveness, which would serve as the ultimate route to improved living standards.

Steering the PCI away from an oppositional, demand-making stance, this imposed a radical reframing of its priorities. As recently as 1975, PCI man and Italian General Confederation of Labour (CGIL) union leader Luciano Lama had signed an accord with employers' federation chief Gianni Agnelli, which bound wage levels to rising inflation, in the attempt to protect purchasing power. But during the period of the historic compromise, Lama reversed course, instead swallowing the so-called 'policy of sacrifices'. This was driven by PCI acceptance of Modigliani's ideas and its desire for alignment with the DC's own budget priorities. In January 1978, Lama lay down the so-called linea dell'EUR, which accepted wage cuts in the interest of 'healing' the economy and boosting growth. The failure of the historic compromise – destroyed in May 1978 when ultra-left terrorists murdered DC party president Aldo Moro – in fact pushed the PCI into a more oppositional stance; after socialist prime minister Craxi imposed a four-point cut in the wage index, in 1985 it attempted to abrogate this move via referendum. But, as historian Guido Liguori writes, there had been a major shift in the PCI's role:

> The greater part of the PCI, still rooted in the country, proudly opposed the repeated attacks coming from its snarling adversaries. It did so above all in the name of defending the 'party tradition' and its existence as a

'community' – the web of relations, solidarity and shared experiences that were built up over time. But large sections of the party, not only in the leadership, from the early 1970s gradually changed political culture and now embraced different political cultures and perspectives. They had become the (subaltern) part of a different hegemonic system.[10]

Taking over the PCI long before its actual dissolution, this turn toward an advocacy of 'sacrifices in the national interest' set in motion a divide within the party's identity. For whereas such a policy reflected a certain vision of labour's stake within Italian capitalism (albeit collapsed into the overall imperatives of Italy's international competitiveness), it cut against the most immediate material demands coming from the working-class base, including the PCI's own activists. In the Berlinguer era the party largely succeeded in reconciling its different souls – in particular, it was as if saved by the fact that it never directly pulled the levers of government, thus deferring any potential splits between the party of *il popolo*, the party of institutional responsibility, the party of the socialist future, and the so-called 'country within a country'. In particular, the collapse of the historic compromise after the murder of Moro both marginalised the PCI relative to the Socialists and pushed it into a more straightforwardly oppositional role. Yet, going further than Liguori, we might point to Berlinguer's embrace of 'morality in politics' in this period as a particular recasting of the left's aims and social categories of reference.

Such a claim should come with caveats. The PCI of the historic-compromise period was more than just a precursor to the neoliberal centre-left, and certain terms it invoked in this period had meanings that cannot simply be reduced to what they later became. When Berlinguer referred, in a famous 1977 speech, to the need to accept 'austerity' as a 'lever to transform Italy', he sought to emphasise that this meant a different set of values to individualistic consumerism, and not simply an offensive against workers' living standards. Yet the overall effect was that the PCI shifted its message onto a terrain of 'morality' that stood in tension or even contradiction with 'material' concerns – whether the louche existence of politicians or the more modest claims of the party's own base. This was a theme powerfully asserted in Berlinguer's 1981 interview with *La Repubblica*'s Eugenio Scalfari, 'Where is the PCI going?' Here, Berlinguer directly linked the idea of 'working-class sacrifices' to the need to rein in the overspending Italian state and the 'advantages' drawn from the parties who ran it.

> [The parties] manage the most disparate and contradictory – sometimes even corrupt – interests without any relation to the rising human needs and demands, or even distorting them, without pursuing the common good . . . [they] have degenerated, to varying degrees, from their constitutional function to serve their own purposes, thus bringing serious damage to both the state and themselves. Yet the Italian Communist Party has not followed them in this degeneration. This is the first reason for our differentness. Do you think Italians ought to be so afraid of this?[11]

Berlinguer's comments would later be taken as a prediction of the failure of the First Republic, casting him in the light of integrity and sobriety while damning that state for its free-spending bureaucratic elephantiasis. This showed the divide between the party's residual strength as a force for republican morality and its difficulty in providing a realistic programme of economic change. After his death on 11 June 1984, Berlinguer became a much-mythologised figure – some 3 million people turned out for his funeral, and the European elections held just six days after his passing brought the PCI to first place in a national election for the first time. Yet if, even at this point, the Communist Party could still win the allegiance of around a third of Italians, both its material base and its identitarian glue were beginning to dissolve. Increasingly cohered by a discourse of 'morality in public life', the PCI was in fact even quicker to move away from a programme of fundamental economic transformations than were forces like François Mitterrand's Parti Socialiste or the UK Labour Party. As its project for changing Italy slipped toward a discourse of combatting inefficiency and bureaucratic waste, the party of Gramsci and Togliatti was beginning to sound more like the liberal critics of Christian Democratic Italy.

What remained difficult, even after the death of a Resistance-era cadre like Berlinguer, was any formal rupture with the PCI's communist identity. Its over 1.5 million members were well versed in party traditions, stretching from Antonio Gramsci to the anti-fascist Resistance and the fight to uproot the Mafia – and it was unclear what exactly might replace it. After a long drift away from both revolutionary aims and Moscow, the end of the PCI would, in fact, require an external trigger. In his day, Berlinguer had declared the spirit of 1917 'exhausted': he sought to preserve the PCI's identity by distancing it from the Soviet Union, even as he also invested hopes in Mikhail Gorbachev's perestroika process. But the failure of reform efforts in the East – and the impressive images of German citizens surmounting the Berlin Wall – inevitably fuelled the belief that the word 'communist' no longer described the reality of the PCI or the project with which it wanted to identify itself. The name change of 1991, however, went far further than just rebadging the party; it radicalised a profound shift in the aims the party was working toward.

The debates on the party's future, evocatively portrayed in Nanni Moretti's 1990 film *La Cosa*, conveyed little sense of what was to come – indeed, the fact that the former PCI would eventually morph into a liberal rather than socialist party, indeed one that primarily based its support on middle-class Italians, was far from apparent in this period. The PDS produced by this process was not yet the PD formed in 2007, or still less the personalised vehicle created by Matteo Renzi in the early part of the following decade. Yet the repudiation of the Communist past had a powerful effect on the cadres of the new party, as did the split by those former members who held on to the old identity. In the PCI, tradition had enjoyed a close connection with both present activity and the socialist future – leading figures like Palmiro Togliatti and Pietro Secchia themselves wrote party histories in order to explain the progress that had been made and to legitimise their decisions. Yet, when this teleology was abandoned and the connection with the future severed, the PCI's epitaph was instead written by figures peripheral or even external to its ranks, such as Lucio Magri in his *Tailor of Ulm*.[12]

The title of Magri's book referred to an intervention during the debates over the PCI's future, in which party stalwart Pietro Ingrao had invoked Bertolt Brecht's parable *1592 Ulm*. The poem, written in 1934 after the defeat of the German labour movement by the Nazis, tells the story of a humble tailor's early attempt at human flight with a set of mechanical wings. When the bold pioneer jumps from the bell tower with his craft only to fall to his death, the ever-cynical bishop tells the watching crowd that his failure had always been inevitable. Yet man would one day fly – and for Ingrao, just the same could be said of the communists. For sure, their first, twentieth-century attempts had crashed to the ground – but why give up on any hope of future success? Impressed by the parable, Magri responded with a few analogies of his own. If the tailor had instead survived, perhaps breaking a few bones, would his friends really have recommended that he try again right away? And if the tailor was right to imagine that human flight was *possible*, what contribution to aeronautics had he actually made?

The answers to such questions were smothered by a narrower debate about identity, in which even the defenders of the name shared few common ideas. Around a third of the delegates to the PCI's final congress, held at Rimini in 1991, rejected the abandonment of its communist identity, and many dissidents then moved to form the PRC together with other far-left forces outside the PCI tradition. In its first decade, Rifondazione was something of a beacon for Europe's radical left – it had some 120,000 activists, regularly scored around 8 per cent of the vote, and showed a particular enthusiasm for social movements. However, while it extolled the merits of pluralism – held as the catch-all response to the failure of the PCI – it never defined a positive identity of its own, beyond the militancy of its 'anti-fascist' opposition to Berlusconi. Lacking a clear governmental agenda, Rifondazione suffered repeated splits over the question of whether to back the neoliberalised centre-left as a temporary block against the billionaire.[13] In 2006, Rifondazione entered government in Romano Prodi's coalition, only to lose all its seats in the subsequent general election.

The repeated splits in Rifondazione, in its failed bid to fully detach itself from PDS, reflected the tumultuous circumstances in which it had first originated. The PCI had over the decades built up an impressive array of local 'sections', and these meeting places were now taken by either PDS or PRC or literally divided down the middle by new iron curtains. The main trade union federation, the CGIL, remained closely aligned to the PDS, but even prominent cadres struggled to pick between the two. Pietro Ingrao, the PCI leadership figure seen as most open to the social movements of the 1970s, initially formed a communist caucus within the PDS before decamping to PRC. The group around the dissident-communist *il manifesto* newspaper took a similar veering path. The most striking example of the upheaval (although admittedly an outlier) was Maria Fida Moro, a senator and daughter of Aldo Moro, the former Christian Democrat premier murdered by the Red Brigades, who defected from her father's party to PRC and then to the neofascist Italian Social Movement.

The split also had a serious disorienting effect on the PCI's former activist base. There had been significant setbacks already in its last decade – from 1980 to 1989 its membership slipped from 1.79 million to 1.42 million, and in 1990, after the fall of the Berlin Wall, this figure fell to 1.26 million. Yet, after the traumatic split of 1991, the decline accelerated – by 1992 the PDS and PRC together counted just 887,455 members. In that year's general election, their combined 21.7 per cent of the vote (representing 8.5 million Italians) fell far short of the PCI's result at its last outing in 1987, when its 10.2 million votes (26.6 per cent) had already been considered a heavy defeat. But something else had also started to disappear. Moretti's *La Cosa* put on display both the profound confusion that followed the end of Soviet socialism and a large-scale mobilisation, as members from around Italy had their say in the local meetings that preceded the party's 'turn'. Yet the split and the PDS's 'liberalisation' replaced this mass democracy with direction by economists and technocrats – including ones who had long stood opposed to the PCI.

This profound shift in the party's priorities, after the name change, was already apparent in one of the first tests of the PDS. In 1992–93, first Giuliano Amato's government and then the administration led by former Bank of Italy governor Carlo Azeglio Ciampi slashed public spending and removed the index that tied wages to inflation: as Giacomo Gabbuti puts it, the effect was to 'dismantle the policies that had allowed the reduction of inequalities and the fairer distribution of the fruits of the postwar "economic miracle" across class and geographical divides'.[14] These measures were swallowed by CGIL union leaders aligned to the PDS, who on 31 July 1992 agreed to abandon wage indexing (keeping salaries ahead of price rises), all in the name of cutting inflation. The offensive was completed that same autumn, as Amato's 'Blood and Tears' budget cut 93 trillion lire (around €49 billion) from the public deficit. This sparked a storm of protest, with mass mobilisations that spread far beyond the control of the confederal union leaders. Yet the parties of government as well as the PDS held firm, with PRC distinguishing itself precisely through its opposition to these moves.

The formation of Ciampi's cabinet provided a farcical display of the PDS's changed imperatives. The first republican administration to be led by an unelected figure, the former bank chief was the first premier since 1947 to include former Communist ministers alongside Socialists and DC figures. Liberated from the *conventio ad excludendum*, which had barred it from national government in the Cold War era, Ciampi tasked former PCI figures with central roles in his austerity administration. In particular, he appointed to the key finance ministry Vincenzo Visco, an independent elected on PCI lists, who had also played a past institutional role in DC administrations. However, while the PDS accepted the basic budget-cutting thrust of the Ciampi administration, in the name of cleaning up the public finances, the party was faced with news on the night of the government's formation that its newfound allies planned to block the prosecution of Bettino Craxi. Just ten hours after Ciampi had welcomed them into his coalition, the PDS's ministers all abandoned their posts.

The 'Need' for Austerity

Italy is heavily in debt – today its €2.4 trillion debt stands above 130 per cent of GDP, and it spends far more on servicing the interest than it does on public education. In this context, austerity measures could either be seen as a means of pushing down the debt or could be criticised as insufficient to 'overcome the country's structural problems'.[15] Yet this picture of a free-spending Italian state sinking ever deeper into debt is rather complicated if we consider the fact that, since 1991, Italian governments have consistently run a primary surplus – that is, they receive more in tax revenues than they spend, prior to interest payments. Italians certainly don't feel like they are frittering their money away – indeed, according to a 2015 report by Eurostat,[16] in real terms they are getting poorer. Taking a base index of 100 for all EU countries, from 2004 Italy fell from 110 (slightly more purchasing power than average) to 96, whereas Germany rose from 120 to 124. For three decades, Italian governments have been cutting public spending and deregulating employment rights, but the effect in undermining domestic demand has actually pushed the debt up.

This development is especially intertwined with the European Economic and Monetary Union (EMU). The fact that even Italian partisans of EMU called it an 'external bind' gives some sense of how it came about – not simply a force that imposed itself from the outside, but rather a set of rules that elites sought in order to restructure Italy. EMU was a matter not only of notes and coins but also of the rules imposed in the Maastricht Treaty, authored by neoliberal economists like Modigliani pupil Tommaso Padoa-Schioppa. Inspired by the liberal triumphalism that greeted the end of the Cold War, this February 1992 treaty provided the ideological framing for the economic restructuring that followed the death of the First Republic. If postwar West Germany had been built on ordoliberalism – a set of fiscal rules that stood above democratic challenge – this order was now extended not only to the newly integrated East but also to countries like Italy. Even beyond the fact that Rome would have to keep public spending within Maastricht deficit limits, in moments of crisis it would no longer rely on a central bank accountable to democratic politicians, but instead to the European Central Bank.

The EMU was never just a 'pooling' of sovereignty among national governments: rather, its own rules imposed a specific economic agenda. The first step was the European Monetary System (EMS) created in 1979, a system of 'semi-fixed' exchange rates in which the lira was allowed to move 6 per cent above or below a central rate defined by the West German mark. The left and trade unions strongly opposed this constraint: in the debates of December 1978, prominent PCIer Giorgio Napolitano warned that as long as the Bundesbank in Frankfurt held to its nonexpansive policy, a country with a weaker currency like Italy would be pushed into deflation.[17] The risk was that (semi-)fixed exchange rates would stop the mark from appreciating but make the lira more expensive, thus imposing wage suppression in order to maintain Italy's international competitiveness. Unless Italy could somehow maintain a higher level of investment and growth, the effect of monetary union would not be to make its economy more like Germany's, but rather to intensify the disparities between them, pushing Italy into constant 'internal devaluation' – reducing labour costs to keep its exports competitive.

As Thomas Fazi and Bill Mitchell have intelligently argued, these widely predicted effects of joining EMS served more as a motivation than a deterrent for Italian elites.[18] In the 1970s, Italy had combined high growth with a strong labour movement, making workers' wages among the highest in Europe in real terms. Joining EMS – and thus the loss of Treasury control over the central bank – imposed internal devaluation, however, while also leaving the Italian public finances increasingly vulnerable to speculation on private debt markets. This meant a shift from a wage-based economy, in which growth was driven by internal demand, to one based on debt and the collection of rents – indeed, from 1976 to 2016, labour incomes dropped from 66 per cent of GDP to just 53 per cent. In Cédric Durand's terms, in subordinating wages to the demands of financial stability, European integration served as the instrument through which capital free[d] itself of a class compromise, relatively favorable to labor, inherited from the postwar period, at the same time as it restructure[d] itself the better to insert itself within globalization and take the road of financialization that was already begun on the other side of the Atlantic.[19]

The claim that Italy would benefit hinged on the notion that (semi-)fixing the lira to the mark would allow it to 'borrow' stability and investor confidence, while greasing the wheels of intra-European trade.[20] Yet as finance minister Giuliano Amato noted in 1988, EMS in fact benefited the countries with the strongest currencies (which were kept artificially cheap) while undermining Italy's own historic growth model, based on high domestic demand.[21] This was bad news for workers in Europe's second-largest manufacturing sector. But the fact that this was an 'external bind' – the apparently 'natural' pressure on the lira from bond markets, which the Treasury was powerless to control – provided the pretext to push through wage cuts in order to combat inflation, as if this was merely an effect of the operation of the free market. The choice to relinquish monetary sovereignty had been just that: a choice. Combined with the free movement of capital, entrenched by the Single European Act of 1986, the effect was to make the entire Italian economy more vulnerable to financial speculation.

If EMS imposed external discipline on Italy's finances, the effect was opposite to what the partisans of fiscal austerity had claimed. Throughout the 1980s, the demands of keeping interest rates above a Bundesbank-imposed 'floor' instead saw a massive rise in the public debt, which soared from 58 to 102 per cent of GDP, even as wages and public spending fell. This was dramatised after German reunification in October 1990, as massive German spending on the integration of the East (accompanied by a huge wave of international investment in German bonds) led the Bundesbank to push up its own interest rates to 10 per cent. As Italy's debt exploded, in June 1992 former treasury minister Giuliano Amato was appointed to form a new government that promised 30 trillion lira (€15 billion) in austerity measures; the Bank of Italy took double that amount from its foreign reserves to buy up lira, in order to try and stabilise the exchange rate. But, faced with massive speculation by George Soros, on 16 September Italy had no choice but to quit the EMS. Having tumbled out of the pseudo-fixed rate system, the lira instantly fell by 20 per cent.

On the same day as Italy quit the EMS, Britain experienced its own 'Black Wednesday', a humiliating experience for John Major's Conservative government. In Britain's case, this prompted a permanent break with the project for a single European currency. In Rome as in London, the fact of crashing out of the EMS was perceived as a political disaster, even though devaluation in fact had many positive consequences. Italy's interest rates now fell below their previous, German-defined levels, and 1993 saw exports boom as the economy received what Fazi calls a 'gulp of oxygen'.[22] As Joseph Halevi writes, the positive effect was limited by the price rises imposed by business.[23] Yet, amid the liberal revolution that followed Clean Hands, the dominant political forces drew the opposite lesson from this episode, holding that exit from the EMS was punishment for Italy's backwardness and the debts racked up by the rotten parties of the First Republic. But this latter was a problem that had built only over the last few years, in which pressure to keep up interest rates had made lira-denominated debt continually more expensive, while cutting the ground from underneath growth.

That little mattered to the champions of the 'external bind'. As they explicitly argued in a hailstorm of books, articles and interventions on national broadcasters, EMU was an instrument for changing Italy itself – what a 1996 work by *La Repubblica*'s Federico Rampini approvingly termed *Germanizzazione*. Where many spoke of European 'integration', implying a compromise among the different nations, Rampini instead championed 'Germanisation' , referring to the use of monetary union as a means of forcing through breakneck privatisations. For a text by a self-described left-winger, this book was remarkably sanguine about the prospect of austerity – the author was unabashed in portraying a future of lower wages, rising unemployment, mounting North–South divides, and restricted democratic control – all justified by the demands of breaking up the old and unloved bureaucratic Italy. A further book saw this same writer in dialogue with then-European commissioner Mario Monti, who stated, without compunction, that if such measures were pushed from the Commission in Brussels rather than Rome itself, they would be 'more sheltered from the electoral process', thus allowing 'Europe to serve Italy's interests, even against its own will'.[24] As prime minister of a cabinet of unelected technocrats 2011–13, Monti would follow this prescription to the letter.

Liberalisation

The politics of the 'external bind' and 'fiscal discipline' marked a historic rupture between the centre-left and its historic social base. In the 1996 election campaign, Romano

Prodi promised that the sacrifices would all be worth it in the end – he insisted that 'with the euro, we'll be working a day less and earning as if we were working a day more'. The real results have fallen far short of this promise. In fact, Italy's GDP per capita has fallen since 1999, with its industrial capacity falling by 25 per cent in this same period. While obedience to 'fiscal discipline' has given Italy primary surpluses every year but one since 1991 – an embrace of austerity without parallel in Europe – and the state has sold off over €110 billion of public assets, interest has pushed the public debt up to €2.4 trillion. This drama is heightened by the lack of industrial policy, as Italy instead asset-strips its economy in the name of an unpayable debt. In 1992, when the debt/GDP ratio surpassed 103 per cent, Prime Minister Amato declared a 'dramatic emergency in the public finances', which called for a 'Blood and Tears' austerity budget. By 2018, this same ratio had reached 135 per cent.[25]

If the rhetoric of liberalisation suggested that Italy was being delivered up to the 'natural' workings of the free market, by cutting away such encumbrances as wage index-ing and collective bargaining, this process was driven by deliberate political choices. When economists like Padoa-Schioppa wrote the Maastricht rules, they were making particular interventions of their own, which barred any future government from a fiscal policy based on borrowing to invest or (in effect) allowing wage rises to drive domestic demand. The choices taken for granted by this framework and embraced by the centre-left were just as 'ideological' as anything that the PCI had ever proposed, as they embraced a drastic shrinking of the public realm in the name of 'liber-alisation'. Yet they also benefited from the aura of 'inevitabil-ity' conferred by the fact they were attached to inalterable

European constraints. Indeed, the PDS's will to transform the First Republic's economic order was also married to a certain cultural disposition toward Italian democracy, considered a source of undue demands that had to be tamed by the 'external bind'.

All major parties with the exception of PRC supported both EMU and this privatisation agenda. But the centre-left especially identified with the single currency, and during its spell in government in 1996 to 2001 it did the legwork for preparing the public finances for Eurozone membership. The 'Mattarellum' electoral law, enacted by the Ciampi government in September 1993, favoured the formation of two broad electoral coalitions, and throughout the period of euro entry the PDS was part of the l'Ulivo alliance led by former Goldman Sachs consultant Romano Prodi. As president of public investment body IRI (Istituto per la Ricostruzione Industriale, National Reconstruction Institute) in the 1980s, Prodi had sold off the state's steel firms, its civil engineering branch, and car maker Alfa Romeo; re-appointed to this same role by Ciampi in 1993, he continued this asset stripping, including the 2 trillion lira (€10 billion) sale of the food wing of state energy firm SME to Unilever. Becoming the centre-left's first prime minister in 1996, Prodi's central policy was to drastically reduce public spending, using the sell-off of state companies (energy, telecoms, Alitalia), as well as cuts in services in order to keep the deficit within EMU limits.

In this sense, the 'external bind' allowed the centre-left to mount a revolution both in its own politics and in the structures of the Italian economy. For the leaders of l'Ulivo, this was not just a matter of cutting spending, but of turning Italy into a 'normal country' free of bureaucracy and its 'blocked' labour market. With Bribesville and Silvio Berlusconi serving as his foil, already in 1994 Prodi had issued *Governing Italy: Manifesto for Change*, a short book in which he advocated that the centre-left take the lead in slimming down the Italian state where the right had failed. Describing 'the light state' as 'the fundamental element of any modern economic policy', Prodi argued for the stripping back of the 'overbearing weight of the public sector', to be achieved through breakneck privatisations and the removal of trade-union bargaining power. Former National Reconstruction Institute (IRI) chief Prodi portrayed public companies not as a potential force for directing growth and maintaining employment, but merely as an inefficient 'state monopoly'. In this vein, he attacked Berlusconi and his far-right partners in Alleanza Nazionale for their lack of energy in conducting privatisations, unduly treating the state as the 'proprietor' of parts of the economy.[26]

Armed by such ideas as well as a heartfelt commitment to Europe, the centre-left pushed economic 'liberalisation' even more aggressively than did Berlusconi. Prodi's language of the 'light state' – and the replacement of state 'welfarism' with a leaner public realm more 'compatible with fiscal imperatives' – was allied to a broader repudiation of the First Republic and its legacy. Telling were the comments by Paolo Flores d'Arcais, a leading anti-Berlusconi activist and editor of current affairs journal *MicroMega*, who had begun his political life as a Trotskyist. His contribution to Prodi's manifesto raised the pseudo-'68er slogan 'Be utopian, demand the possible' as he called for the 'revolution of normality, of Western normality' to sweep across a land defined by backwardness and criminality. Accompanied by a call for Italians to mount a 'revolution in seriousness' and a 'revolution in legality', Flores d'Arcais interpreted both Bribesville and Berlusconism as examples of Italy's deep cultural deficit. In the new liberals' thinking, this would be overcome by embracing such paragons of public morality as the European Union and Bill Clinton, now anointed hero of the ex-Communist liberal left.

Such liberalisation was, indeed, the ideological glue for the first government of the centre-left. This began even during the 1996 election campaign, as Prodi called for 'eighteen months of cuts and sacrifices in order to heal Italy',[27] and after assuming office on 18 May, his entire policy was directed to meeting the 3 per cent deficit ceiling set out by Maastricht. With the PDS's Visco as finance minister and Ciampi in the Treasury, Prodi used all means at hand to slash the public deficit, from an offensive against tax evasion to the sell-off of the state tobacco monopoly, a raft of austerity measures and even a one-off tax called the Extraordinary Contribution for Europe, 60 per cent of which would be repaid the following year. Aided by such fixes, within six months Prodi had succeeded in reducing the deficit from 3.2 to 2.7 per cent. Yet at the same time, he also signed Italy up to an even tighter 'external bind'. In July 1997, the EMU states sealed a Stability and Growth Pact, which granted the European Commission and Council of Ministers 'surveillance' over economies, including Italy's, in which public debt amounted to more than 60 per cent of GDP. This included the power to fine national governments or even impose its own policies over their heads.

In this embrace of the free market (framed by the budget-clenching limits of the European project) the idea of representing a distinct labour interest rapidly dissipated. This was especially notable in the Treu reform of 1997, which promoted short-term contracts in the interest of creating instability and thus competition in the labour market. Indeed, this ideology of deregulation spanned the different traditions united in l'Ulivo, far beyond career technocrats like Ciampi and Prodi. For instance, Pier Luigi Bersani – a former member of the extra-parliamentary left who joined the PCI and then the PDS, and later became a left-wing critic of Matteo Renzi – was Prodi's industry minister, in which role he spearheaded the privatisation of the publicly owned electricity company. When Rifondazione finally withdrew its support from Prodi in October 1998, this led to a new government (backed by a split from PRC named PdCI) in which PDS leader Massimo d'Alema became premier. Yet the change in political personnel – bringing an ex-Communist to power in a NATO country for the first time – did not prompt a change of agenda. With Prodi moved to the European Commission, D'Alema pursued the same privatisation programme and moreover registered the PDS's backing for the Atlantic Pact by joining the Western intervention in Yugoslavia.

Just weeks after D'Alema became prime minister, Italy joined the currency union as scheduled on 1 January 1999, a success lauded across most of the political mainstream. Despite Berlusconi's later criticisms of 'Prodi's euro' or, indeed, the centre-left's own bid to define itself against Forza Italia on this terrain, upon the single currency's launch the billionaire had instead tried to claim part of the credit. This was especially notable after he returned to the prime minister's office in 2001. As Italians prepared to begin using euro notes and coins on 1 January 2002, Berlusconi sent a conversion calculator to every household, accompanied by a signed letter vaunting the merits of the single currency. But the 'external bind' had not only imposed new imperatives on the Italian economy, but also reshaped the aspirations of the centre-left. In its role at the heart of l'Ulivo, the PDS had turned the old 'policy of sacrifices' into a call to do anything necessary to meet eurozone budget criteria. Recycling institutional figures like Ciampi, Dini, Prodi, and Amato (who enjoyed a fresh spell as prime minister in 2000–2001), through its first five years in government the centre-left adopted the language of the 'revolution in seriousness' – the 'politics of two stages' in which immediate sacrifices would prepare the way for future well-being.

The problem, in terms of the centre-left's electoral fortunes, is that the much-vaunted future well-being has never actually come. Rather, the commitment to Europe has instead become a kind of cultural signifier standing above measurable material interest – indeed, one increasingly decisive for the centre-left's political identity. President of the republic at the moment that Italy abandoned the lira in 2002, Ciampi spoke for many on the centre-left when he heralded the new currency as a vision of the kind of country Italy could be. He extolled its creation as a 'historic event', 'the realization of a dream', synonymous with healing the economy, monetary stability, low interest rates, the transparency of goods and services, and thus greater freedom for consumers, but above all 'the birth of Europe as a political subject'.[28] This vision was shared by long-time PCI *migliorista* Giorgio Napolitano, whose book *Political Europe* extolled the merits of the European project but damned the left's long-standing criticisms of it. Since the signing of the Treaty of Rome in 1957, the PCI had opposed European integration, seeing it as a cartel of capitalist states beholden to business interests. Napolitano did not deign to address this particular claim, but rather insisted that the First Republic had shown Italy's supposed lack of 'cultural and political depth', which could now instead be found at the superior European level.[29]

At that time blindly accepted by all mainstream media, today the claims of these scions of the centre-left appear as not merely pompous, but richly ironic. Where in the 1970s the Communist Napolitano pointed to the dangers that the currency union posed to working-class living standards, two decades later he ardently defended the sacrifices that blue-collar Italy would have to make in the name of loyalty to the European project. However intransigently Italy's techno-cratic elites hold to such dogmas, the consequences have proven nothing short of disastrous, for working-class living standards, for growth, and for Italians' connections to their own democratic institutions. As we shall see, in the eurozone era Italy has not only suffered protracted economic woes, but its population has passed from being among the most Euro-federalist countries to among the Eurosceptic. Polls in 2018 showed that the Italian population is even more unhappy with the EU than the Britons who voted for Brexit[30] – and it blames the centre-left for its troubles. As Napolitano's own trajectory shows, the left's journey from PCI to PD was, indeed, far more than a name change.

3

A Country for Old Men

'I didn't ever plan on entering politics', Silvio Berlusconi declared at the start of 2018, as he headed into his seventh successive general election campaign. A quarter century earlier, he had appeared as an innovator, using his private TV empire as a winning campaigning platform; now, in the era of the internet, the eighty-one-year-old once again put his name forth in the name of renewal. His previous removal from high office in 2011 had, after all, owed to an even more venerable figure – President Giorgio Napolitano, already eighty-six years old when he brought an end to the last Berlusconi-led government. These are but two prominent faces in a gerontocratic society – one in which men well past the retirement age are at the heart of all fields of public life, from politics to media, business, and academia.

Doubtless, one of the first things that strikes any observer of Italian society is the pervasive gerontocracy. The idea of 'youth' extends well into what Britons would consider middle age – and not only because, as a travel writer's vision of the world might put it, lashings of olive oil are pushing up Italians' life expectancy. In today's Italy, some three-quarters of university students live with their parents, and most adults up to age thirty-five years remain in the family home. Worse, they are treated even by their elected officials as eternal children – including by what passes for the centre-left. The PD's Giuliano Poletti, minister of labour from 2014 to 2018, remarked that he was glad that Italians were leaving the country rather than 'getting under the feet' of their parents. In this he followed the example of crisis-era welfare secretary Michel Martone, a member of Mario Monti's technocratic government, who deemed the typical twenty-eight-year-old outside of work or study a 'loser'.[1]

Italians who are Not in Education, Employment or Training (NEET) in fact represent an ever-growing portion of the population. According to 2019 Eurostat figures, 28.9 per cent of Italians between ages twenty and thirty-four are NEETs, making this the single worst-performing European country – Sicily is Europe's single worst-performing region (38.6 per cent NEETs) followed by Calabria (36.2 per cent) and Campania (the region surrounding Naples, 35.9 per cent). As well as lying far behind the EU average (16.5 per cent), Spain (19.6 per cent), and Greece (26.8 per cent), Italy's figures have also worsened in the post-crisis period, in tandem with the fall in job opportunities for eighteen-to-twenty-four-year-olds. Indeed, the share of young adults classified as jobseekers reached 42.7 per cent in 2014, near double pre-crisis levels. This is making them more dependent on their families, and not only for housing. Since 2008, the number of Italians between twenty-five and thirty-four years of age who live with their parents has gone up by 10 per cent, rising to 51 per cent of the total.

If we responded like many centrist politicians, we could conclude that Italy has a high concentration of 'mummy's boys' still tied to the apron strings – a culture that must be deep-rooted indeed in the aforementioned regions. Yet one might then ask why the number of young Italians who are moving in search of work – especially from the unemployment-hit South – is today reaching historic highs. A 2018 Svimez study showed that, between 2000 and 2016, some 1,882,872 southerners left their home regions behind, largely in favour of north-central Italy or other European countries. Since the 2008 crisis, the total rate of emigration *from* Italy has, in fact, soared to between 250,000 and 300,000 people a year – figures unseen since the great wave of interregional and international migration that marked the immediate post-1945 period.[2]

The notion that young Italians are simply too lazy or picky to find employment is, most visibly, belied by the large numbers doing unenviable jobs as home-care workers and cooks in cities like London and Berlin. Yet the political debate back home – with its special poison for another kind of migrants, those reaching Italy – is consistently confused by the 'labour lump fallacy', namely the assumption that there is a fixed number of jobs available in the economy, to which the job-seeking population must therefore adapt itself or be adapted. This is not only the illusion of those on the populist right who insist on the need to prevent other people joining the labour market (thus stopping migrants from 'taking our jobs'). It also informs centrist analyses which claim that the problem lies in the job stability of older workers – 'shutting out' young Italians – or else the lack of industrious spirit among the young themselves.

The dominance of such analyses points to a deep cultural pessimism, in which it seems impossible for Italians to do more than share existing scarce resources. This view is doubtless fed by the sheer longevity of Italy's ills, which long predate the 2008 crisis. In towns that have suffered high unemployment for three decades or more, a common-sense reading might easily conceptualise a zero-sum game in which there are 'not enough jobs to go around', or focus on the presumed cultural divide separating the go-getting youth of past decades from their lazier, more homebound successors in the present. Yet even those political interventions that speak of pushing more youngsters into work consistently centre on the idea of 'flexibilising' the labour market. In this analysis, bosses (today rebranded 'job-givers') will be more willing to hire young people on a short-term basis if they know this will not lumber them with long-term costs.

Such an idea fits a widespread liberal conception of over-indulged workers creating blockages on the labour market. Telling was the social-media spread, in 2014, of the story of the 'Jazz Miner' – a worker who admitted spending almost his whole career faking illness so that he could stay at home listening to jazz music.[3] Circulating at the very moment that youth unemployment peaked, this meme conformed to a popular view of Italy as a land where old-fashioned labour laws keep layabouts in their posts, at the expense of both their bosses and others who want to enter the labour market. This is, certainly, the message hammered home by the partisans of labour-market reform. Yet the paradox is that the Organisation for Economic Co-operation and Development (OECD) counts Italy as the country that has done most to 'flexibilise' its labour market since the 1990s.[4] A series of reforms have made short-term contracts the norm – with the effect that since 2000 the proportion of young workers hired on term-limited contracts has soared from 26 per cent to 67 per cent of the total.[5]

Such 'flexibilisation' has nothing to do with creating more job opportunities or removing the overall fetters to economic growth. Not only has the bid to create more competition in the labour market been unable to compensate for a general slow-down in job creation, given the climate of steeply falling investment, but it has been part and parcel of a generalised offensive against working-class living standards. There is simply no empirical evidence that making contracts more precarious increases the overall level of employment in the economy; and absent such growth, 'flexibilisation' does nothing but reduce workers' ability to count on the employment they have already. Anti-EU discourse in Britain often focuses on the idea of 'red tape' imposed by Brussels – senseless rules that unduly tie up business. But in Italy it is the European institutions and their local partisans who insist that labour rights are mere bureaucratic hurdles, which stand in the way of the 'liberalisation' that the single currency seeks to impose.

In Chapter 2, we noted the decline in the political discourse of solidarity and collective solutions. This is most obvious at the level of organised politics, in the changed priorities of a neoliberal left unbound from its historic social base. Yet the weakening of this political glue matches a broader fragmentation of working-class Italy: indeed, the atomised and precarious are unlikely to have a strong sense of class identification, if they are forever competing with others for scraps of work. But even as the face of labour changes, the Italy of more recent decades – with its falling investment and worsening workplace conditions – has also cohered new kinds of class divides, at the nexus of age, education, employment, and property ownership. While the young are struggling to make their careers in Italy – forced into the position of precarious job seekers, who increasingly either live with their parents or emigrate – their older and more propertied fellow citizens are taking up an ever-higher share of national income, based on rent.

If Italy has a particularly fragmented class structure, with a high proportion of self-employed, the woeful situation of recent years owes not to some eternal cultural condition but to specific political choices. Indeed, even as Italians' life prospects worsen, any hope of kick-starting productive investment – and thus creating more job opportunities – has remained subordinate to the dogma of budget cutting, whether at the level of the private firm or in the austerity imposed from central government. This situation has worsened further since the 2008 crisis, with the abject failure to take countercyclical measures that might have broken with the dogma of austerity. Leading a technocratic cabinet at the height of the European crisis in 2011–13, former Goldman Sachs advisor Mario Monti admitted to CNN that 'fiscal consolidation' had served to 'destroy domestic demand' – the payoff would supposedly come in terms of 'international competitiveness' that would eventually come from being able to sell cheaper Italian goods elsewhere in Europe.[6]

Such an agenda has won centrist parties few admirers among young Italians. The mantra of permanent austerity, enforced even during periods of crisis and falling demand, has instead turned the Italian economy into a theatre of asset stripping, in which public goods are sold off and only the private owners of real estate are able to push up their incomes, especially thanks to tourism and Airbnbs. The fact that this agenda has been imposed regardless of the immediate economic circumstances merely illustrates the intensely ideological nature of this project, carried through even at the cost of increasing the debt burden and undermining the bases of future growth. This nihilism, unable even to offer some future payoff in exchange for the sacrifices of the present, has pulverised living standards and undermined Italians' bind to democratic politics. More liberal than their parents in their social mores and more likely to go to university, young Italians are also more Eurosceptic, less engaged with parties or trade unions, and less likely to vote. They, not the older and richer citizens who make up the Lega's core base, are the true 'left behind' of the Second Republic.

Earlier we looked at the worsening fortunes of young Italians and the associated rise of the discourse of 'managed decline'. It is true that Italy faced economic problems long before the 2008 crisis or even its entrance into the single currency in 1999 – and as we have said, it is also doing worse than other European countries. Yet the constraints imposed at the European level also prevent Italy from doing anything to reduce its vast €2.4 trillion national debt and have also left it no means of restoring growth except to pursue an 'internal devaluation' – that is, to become more competitive on international markets by slashing wages. In this chapter, we see how the political dogmas of the Second Republic, allied to the constraints of eurozone membership, have systematically prevented any recovery or even the paying off of the debt, pushing Italy deeper into the hole of wage cutting, mass unemployment, and 'fiscal consolidation'. These choices have, in short, imposed a historic fall in popular living standards and the life prospects of the young.

No Future to Invest in

We are interested in young people's economic prospects – how their conditions and expectations have changed in new political circumstances. But the normal invocation of the generational question in Italian public life has more to do with demography, narrowly conceived – an obsession with declining birth rates, taken as a symptom of national decline. In autumn 2016 the PD-led government proclaimed a so-called Fertility Day, in a bid to highlight this issue. It issued a series of advertisements that combined public-health messages about the harmful effects of substance abuse with rather cruder exhortations for couples to stop 'waiting for the stork' and 'get moving'. In July 2017 Patrizia Prestipino, a member of the PD's national leadership, called for 'support for mothers' to avoid the 'extinction' of the 'Italian race'. When, in August 2018, Luigi Di Maio announced plans to give workers more stable contracts, he announced that this stability was necessary in order 'to help them have kids.'[7]

Such interventions especially fed on the narrative that there is too high a proportion of pensioners – a millstone around the neck of those who work and pay taxes. It is not quite true, as Lega leader Umberto Bossi claimed in 2017, that each worker is paying for a pensioner – according to April 2018 Italian National Institute of Statistics (ISTAT) figures, Italy has marginally over 16 million pensioners (around 500,000 of whom are also employed), well beneath the 23.2 million people in work.[8] But all evidence suggests that this ratio is set to narrow over the next few decades, as baby boomers become older. According to the Ragioneria generale della Stato (which uses a slightly narrower definition of pensioners than ISTAT), by 2050 the retired population will have risen to 17.5 million, while the number of Italians in work will have fallen to 22 million.[9] The overall population is set to shrink over the next three decades, but a larger share of them will be retired.

This shift in Italian demography, allied to declining birth rates, suggests one of the reasons why citizens have little confidence in the future. Even beyond the epochal worries posed by climate change, why raise children in a country where one is unable to find a steady income or to rely on the state for even basic services? This problem is also magnified by the austerity-era pushing of care responsibilities onto the family itself. Already in the 1990s, the 'natural balance' of births versus deaths (population numbers, unaltered by migration) passed a historic threshold, as the number of Italians who died surpassed the number being born. In the more recent period of economic crisis, this situation has worsened yet further. In 2018, Italy hit a new record low for the number of births: the 453,000 figure marked a drop of over 100,000 from 2008, and for the first time there were more Italians in their eighties than babies. This tells us that the average age will continue to rise at least until the midpoint of the current century.

Yet to decry the sheer numbers of pensioners does not explain what is happening here. Italy has the world's fifth-highest median age (45.4 years), around four years higher than Britain or France. But this is actually lower than the average age in far-better-performing Germany (47.1). A closer look at the age structure of the workforce suggests that Italy's problems owe less to purely demographic problems – the number of old people, or low birth rates – than to the failure to provide opportunities for those who *could* be working. Only 62 per cent of Italians between twenty and sixty-four years old are employed: this is the second-lowest figure in Europe, far below Britain (78.2 per cent) and the EU average (72.2 per cent) and barely ahead of Greece (57.8 per cent).[10] Any political discourse that suggests the way to create employment for young Italians is to push older workers out of their jobs, or else to put up barriers to migrants, is a simple distraction from the need to improve the employment rate.

The key reason for low employment is a lack of investment, indeed in multiple fields. This is especially notable in the low female employment rate – 48.8 per cent, one-third lower than the figure for men, and the lowest rate in Europe. As in Britain and Germany, Italian women are vastly over-represented among part-time workers (32.8 per cent of women in employment work part-time, as opposed to 8 per cent of employed men), but the overall gender employment gap is twice as high. This especially owes to the lack of state support for mothers, with nursery places for only one in five children under age three.[11] In 2016, 78 per cent of women who quit work were mothers; a Labour Inspectorate study found that of 29,879 women leaving their jobs that year, only 5,261 reported finding new employment, whereas 24,618 left the labour market citing childcare or a 'difficult work–life balance'.[12] Close families and intergenerational solidarity simply aren't picking up the slack. Rather, the gender division of labour in the home, combined with the lack of childcare provision, makes it harder for working women to have children – and for mothers to hold down jobs that fit in with their other responsibilities.

Yet, beyond the lack of public services to help women in work, the climate of falling investment (down more than 40 per cent since 2008) also serves to limit the overall amount of employment in the economy. This problem has, indeed, intensified over recent crises, as the number of Italians who lose their jobs increases and gloomy future prospects discourage businesses from taking on new hires. Austerity policies have played a powerful role in entrenching long-term unemployment or underemployment. Simply put, if Italian businesses stay afloat through recession periods by cutting costs, and the state is unable or unwilling to fill in for the lack of investment, then the overall demand for new hires will fall, and even those jobs that do become available will be disproportionately part-time or otherwise precarious. This also has an effect in depressing wages, which in 2019 still remain below pre-2008 levels. Even among the highly educated, Italian graduate incomes are around half of German levels; Willis Towers Watson's *Global 50 Remuneration Planning Report* ranks Italy last among all Western European countries.[13]

The fact that Italy's wage levels are performing so much worse than other European economies is the result not of natural market developments, or some innate cultural woes, but conscious political choices. At issue here is not a simple relationship of supply and demand, as if unemployment automatically reduced workers' bargaining power, but also the kind of jobs that a low-investment economy is built around, in a period of internal devaluation. There are some exceptions to the rule, in what remains Europe's second-biggest manufacturing economy. The Expo held in Milan in 2015, focused on a celebration of Italy's food industry, was less caricatural than it sounds – the €13 billion show did, after all, focus on sustainable development and new technology in agroindustry rather than just serve up bounteous helpings of Soave and Taleggio. As well as agriculture and food processing, Italy has important islands of modernisation in industries such as machine tool production as well as car manufacturing and biotechnology. Yet drastic regional disparities and low investment mean that overall Italian manufacturing is declining relative to France or Germany, while tourism becomes the only major growth sector.

Externally Bound

This spell of low public investment also owes to the particular limits imposed by Italy's integration into the single currency. Over the 1990s and 2000s, Italian growth was slow, but over the last decade its economy has in fact shrunk. Its failure (or inability) to recover from the 2008 crisis means that total GDP is lower today than it was upon the formation of the eurozone in 1999. Its debt, meanwhile, has grown far higher, as interest rates have outstripped growth. At the level of public investment, the problem particularly owes to the Maastricht Treaty's policing of deficit limits, barring the state from picking up the slack as private investment has fallen. Italian politicians bear their own responsibility for signing up to the treaty – the neoliberal credos it entrenches were much in vogue in the Italy of the early 1990s, as across the West. Yet the decisions made in this period have also imposed a strait jacket on all subsequent governments, hardcoding an unalterable political vision into the rules that determine all future economic policy.

These dynamics were particularly visible in the policies pursued by the European Central Bank (ECB) since 2008, regarding quantitative easing and the sovereign debt. This was particularly notable for the ECB's ability to set the course of Italian labour and social policy, imposing a series of 'reforms' in exchange for short bursts of liquidity. While the ECB does have a certain freedom to issue or deny liquidity, depending on the political will of the day, both the dominant dogmas among European leaders and the treaty rules framing all decisions have imposed a basically intransigent policy course, imposing austerity measures as well as increased 'labour market flexibility' as catch-all solutions to Italian economic ills. While these moves to cut investment and indeed working-class Italians' living standards were the constant of European policy – claimed by Italian elites to be unavoidable medicine for the economy – such alternative solutions as debt relief or increases in public borrowing were ruled out on principle and, indeed, by the treaty. The social emergency created by the crisis counted for nothing compared to the maintenance of Maastricht rules.

Any narrative of external constraint must come with a caution – for the period following the 2008 crisis was hardly a tale of Italian Davids standing up to European Goliaths. Many of the leading personnel in Brussels imposing reforms on the country were Italians, notably ECB chief Mario Draghi, and crisis-era governments in Rome were of similar political hue to those which had delivered previous rounds of austerity. Rather, these events showed how an external bind could be used as an instrument of domestic politics – invoking European demands in order to overrule democratic decision-making in moments of stress. This was especially illustrated in the fate of the government in office in the immediate crisis period, a right-wing coalition led by Silvio Berlusconi. Alongside Portugal, Ireland, Greece, and Spain, Italy was one of the most heavily indebted countries in the eurozone, and in summer 2011 there was intense speculation against its sovereign debt, which sharply pushed interest rates. If Italy had its own currency, the government would have eased the pressure by making the central bank buy up sovereign bonds – but the ECB refused to do this until Rome implemented other economic reforms to its liking.

As Freddie Mac director Rahm Emanuel put it in 2008, one should 'never let a serious crisis go to waste'.[14] For ECB chiefs Jean-Claude Trichet and Mario Draghi, this meant exploiting Italy's vulnerability in order to impose their demands. On 5 August 2011 they sent Berlusconi a letter listing measures he should take to restore investor confidence – in reality, conditions that had to be met before the ECB would itself intervene on the markets.[15] The aim was not to soften the effects of the crisis or even to restore growth, but rather to use this moment to impose a much broader agenda of cutting back the Italian state. ECB demands ranged from 'the full liberalisation of local public services' – including 'large-scale privatisations' – to measures 'significantly reducing the cost of public employees, by strengthening turnover rules and, if necessary, by reducing wages.'[16] This was twinned with moves to cut back sector-level collective bargaining (forcing unions to make deals firm-by-firm, and thus weakening their collective power) and automatic mechanisms which would cut public spending in case of 'slippages' from deficit targets.

Faced with the intense pressure on the bond markets, pushing it toward insolvency, the Berlusconi government was powerless to refuse. As one commentary on the letter put it, the ECB had long promoted privatisation and wage cuts, at least at the level of policy recommendations – now the 'catastrophic bond-market speculation' of summer 2011 provided it a 'failsafe tool' to impose its policy, since it served as a 'gun to the [government's] head . . . that only the ECB could disarm'.[17] The ECB demands did help Berlusconi disarm his domestic opponents, citing European pressure – indeed, just a week after the letter, he reversed the result of a June 2011 referendum that saw a 95 per cent vote to stop the privatisation of local services on a 55 per cent turnout.[18] But plans were in the offing for a rather different solution to Italy's woes – a new, 'nonpolitical' government that would directly take austerity measures in hand. Just as former bank chiefs Ciampi and Dini had pushed through cuts in the 1990s, former Goldman Sachs advisor Mario Monti was now lined up for a similar role.

There is no need here to enter into the many conspiracy theories surrounding Berlusconi's replacement, or indeed to entertain the pretence that he had somehow opposed austerity before Monti was installed. Such resistance never existed. But scheming behind the scenes there certainly was. Over the summer of 2011, parallel to the ECB letter, President Giorgio Napolitano worked together with Draghi and the banker Corrado Passera to prepare a programme of austerity measures for Italy, which were intended to be pushed through by a new cabinet.[19] The unbearable market pressure on Berlusconi, as the spread rose, made it impossible for his government to continue, with the ECB willing to save Italy only after a more 'reliable' cabinet had been installed in its place. Monti was then appointed prime minister in November, with Passera as economy minister, in a cabinet entirely composed of unelected technocrats. Notably, it was backed in parliament not only by the Democrats but also by Berlusconi's Popolo della Libertà, which supported the new technical government.

Created in the name of loyalty to Italy's European partners, this government's programme certainly highlighted the democratic impasse that the country had reached. Supported by the main centre-left and centre-right parties as well as a smattering of smaller allies, the Monti cabinet enjoyed a massive majority in parliament, despite having no popular mandate for the reforms it proposed to enact. There was some opposition – notably the Lega Nord, the newborn Five Star Movement (which was yet to enter parliament) and Italia dei Valori. Yet the government nonetheless rapidly translated ECB plans onto the statute books, unresponsive to the normal imperatives of government performance. Indeed, this technocratic administration's aim was not to restore growth but rather to carry through 'restructuring measures' explicitly aimed at wage reduction and slashing internal demand. For any elected government, taking measures that reduced GDP by 2.4 per cent in its first year in office would have been suicidal. But as Monti explained to CNN, his government's focus on 'fiscal consolidation' stood above any need to alleviate crisis conditions.

From the perspective of unelected technocrats, this government was, indeed, a success, making the best of the crisis to push through measures which Italians would never have backed in an election. There were those who saw this as sacrifices today in exchange for pay-off tomorrow. For leading business daily *Il Sole 24 Ore*, the Trichet-Draghi letter represented continuity with the strategy of eurozone founding fathers Jacques Delors and Tommaso Padoa-Schioppa, implementing a governance regime that would lay the basis for a more stable future growth.[20] Yet it also represented an unprecedented European intervention in the internal affairs of a member state, testing out the mechanisms by which Brussels would soon impose harsh austerity on Greece. The EU's institutions did not waver from Maastricht rules in order to alleviate the effects of crisis, or still less question the ideological assumptions underlying them. Rather, they used the crisis period to imbed disciplining mechanisms deeper into the Italian economy.

Treating Workers as Babies

The Goldman Sachs man Monti typified the recycling of personnel between the worlds of finance, international institutions, and Italian domestic politics – as Perry Anderson points out, it was ironic that a man so linked to the firm who had 'cooked the books' in Greece before it joined the eurozone was now held up as the representative of European propriety. But this case was hardly rare, even in the recent history of the Italian centre-left. After helping to write the rules for the single currency, in 2006–8 former European Commission official Padoa-Schioppa had taken up a more public role in domestic politics, as economy minister in Romano Prodi's government. A student of Franco Modigliani at Massachusetts Institute of Technology, the 'liberal Keynesian' Padoa-Schioppa could occupy such an important office even without ever being elected to any role at all, the important thing being that he was a pro-European committed to the politics of privatisation. Indeed, for him and others, engagement in electoral politics was irrelevant to the 'necessity' of the choices that they were making.

Monti was especially outspoken in defending the more undemocratic aspects of this shift. Indeed, never having been elected to public office, he dismissed critics with grandiloquent remarks on the limits of popular decision making. He admitted that Italians in search of 'short-term fixes' rejected austerity, but he insisted that he would eventually be proven correct. Defending his record in a 2014 address in Paris, Monti quoted US founding father Alexander Hamilton to insist on the supremacy of expertise over democratic politics. As he put it,

> when occasions present themselves, in which the interests of the people are at variance with their inclinations, it is the duty of the persons whom they have appointed to be the guardians of those interests, to withstand the temporary delusion, in order to give them time and opportunity for more cool and sedate reflection.[21]

In fact, he and his ministers had never been appointed by the Italian people as guardians of their interests: his was a cabinet of unelected technocrats whose parliamentary backing depended on parties that had hitherto stood as bitter opponents.

The former Goldman Sachs advisor maintained that his 'mission' would ultimately serve Italians' well-being: fiscal discipline was a 'beneficial cure for the young generations', whose real interests would only be 'sacrificed' by pandering to their own fickle demands. This haughtiness recalled similar comments by Padoa-Schioppa, back when he reported to a parliamentary budget commission on measures to 'incentivise young people to leave their parents' homes'. This administration, unlike Monti's, was mainly staffed by what passed for left-wing parties – as well as the newly created PD, the second leading force was Rifondazione. But the most significant element of Padoa-Schioppa's intervention was the manner in which he chose to describe the supposed beneficiaries of his policy, remarking that the government ought to ensure that *bamboccioni* (big babies who were still sucking on their dummies or pacifiers) stopped being a charge on their parents.

These comments by Padoa-Schioppa, a lifelong bank administrator and European technocrat, were characterised as unfortunate by some of his PD colleagues. Yet they also had the merit of providing an insight into what such technocrats really thought of the population. For such figures, the Italians who complained about the decades-long fall in real wages or mass unemployment had merely demonstrated their lack of seriousness, refusing to swallow a medicine that was being administered in their own best interests. In the crisis period in particular, both institutional figures like these and politicians rising up the ranks of the PD developed a sharp elitist edge, indeed cohering their own electorate on this basis. Faced with a dramatic social crisis, pro-European liberals increasingly embraced their role as gatekeepers of institutional rules, standing up for hard-working Italians against the childish complaints coming from idle young people and 'populist' opposition parties.

This reorientation away from the historic priorities of the left was most starkly illustrated in the field of labour policy, where politicians from across the spectrum have heaped blame on the young for their own failure to find work. From this perspective, it seemed that the lack of young Italians finding work owed not to the measurable and drastic fall in public investment, starving the economy of funds, or indeed the government's publicly stated policy of slashing the labour bill, but, rather, that young jobseekers expected too much. During his premiership, in 2012 Monti claimed that 'young people should drop the idea that they'll get fixed jobs' which were 'boring anyway'. His labour minister Elsa Fornero similarly insisted they shouldn't be 'choosy' about what job they got, while her centre-left successor commented that Italians did not seem 'very employable' or like 'human capital to invest in'. In 2018, Berlusconi offered his own agreement that young people 'wake up at midday, stay in their rooms playing on the computer, eat in the evening then go clubbing'.[22]

These insults certainly illustrate politicians' distance from the young people on the receiving end of recipes like 'fiscal consolidation' and 'destroying domestic demand'. Yet the policies that they accompany are, outwardly at least, aimed at improving young people's situation, helping to drive them out of their precocious lassitude and into a more active existence. Indeed, the labour-market measures pursued by all governments in recent decades – starting with the centre-left's Treu reform in 1997 and the Lega-backed Biagi-Maroni law of 2003 – have spoken of making more space for young workers. The point, it is said, is to remove the exaggerated protections that supposedly keep their older counterparts in jobs for life – protections unfairly prioritising those lucky enough to have hit on stable employment already. Beyond deriding fixed job posts as 'boring', Monti also insisted on the need to end what he called the 'apartheid' between those protected by labour legislation and the young people on short-term contracts.

Italian liberals often tell us they want public life to be a show of hard-headed seriousness, rather than home to the insults and empty invective proffered by the likes of Berlusconi or the Five Star Movement. Yet they mustered little energy to condemn Monti's comparison between racial exclusion and the legal codes that protect Italian workers from unfair dismissal (and indeed, discrimination of all kinds). Instead, upon its return to government after the

February 2013 general election, the PD adopted Monti's call as its own, targeting Article 18 of the 1970 Workers' Statute as representative of the bureaucratic impediments that foster youth unemployment. Presenting himself as the 'demolition man' on the crusade against elderly elites, upon becoming prime minister in 2014 the youthful premier Matteo Renzi moved to roll back a historic conquest of Italian trade union-ism, which even Berlusconi had shied from dismantling.

Typical of the elitist craze to see all things Italian as backward and all things Anglophone as modern, Renzi's move to eviscerate the Workers' Statute appeared with an English name: the Jobs Act, passed in 2015. Though this bill had the explicit intention of stimulating employment, it followed the same basic ideological pattern as the other 'liberalisation' measures which had passed by previous governments, shifting the balance of workplace power to the advantage of employers while also dismantling historic labour rights in the name of 'flexibility'. The Jobs Act promised to reward 'job-givers' in workplaces of over fifteen staff by offering tax cuts for short-term contracts and legalising 'sackings without just cause', thus loosening legal obligations to employees. This also marked the final split between Renzi's PD and the CGIL (Italian General Confederation of Labour) trade union, which saw the move as a direct attack on labour rights.

Like the Treu reform of 1997, the PD prime minister's Jobs Act promised to increase overall employment by provid-ing a legal framework for casual and fragmented work patterns. For its supporters, Renzi's reform had a bigger impact than its predecessors: his allies like economist Tito Boeri trumpeted the success of the 2015 reform, alleged to have created 'one million jobs' within its first year. In fact, the total increase in employment over the next period was far more modest – 800,000 in three years – and was dubiously attributable to the reform itself. Indeed, not only did this small sign of recovery keep the absolute number of Italians in work below 2008 levels, but this also represented a smaller proportion of the total population, which had in the meantime grown by 2 million people.[23] Even aside from the actual reason why jobs were created, it is also worth noting their low quality – close to half of them are short-term posts.

One of the most alarming developments in this regard has been the rise of 'labour vouchers', introduced into law by the right-wing government in 2003 with the Biagi-Maroni law. Issued in the name of combatting black-market labour as well as encouraging the regularisation of underprivileged groups (including women), payment by vouchers redeemable at post offices and tobacconists was supposed to put ready-taxed wages directly into workers' hands. Yet these payments are in fact a way around providing a contract – usable for up to thirty days, they are not bound to employment rights of any kind. Marta Fana, author of a renowned recent study of youth exploitation, cites the case of a twenty-three-year-old paid by such vouchers who lost three fingers in a workplace injury. He received no sick pay and indeed did not 'need' to be sacked, because he had never been properly hired to begin with.[24] When they first came into use in 2008, the government sold 50,000 of these €10 labour vouchers to employers; this figure had reached 24 million by 2012 and 69 million by 2014.[25]

In short, the effect of post-crisis policies has been to undermine unemployment security, the paid value of work, and job-creating investment, while pushing a moralistic rhetoric that criticises young people for failing to get a job and old people for keeping one. As befitting this culture of blame, Renzi's *alternanza scuola-lavoro* (school-to-work alternation) initiative turned unpaid employment into an obligation on all high-school students. Grammar schoolers would now have to put in 200 hours a year unpaid employment, and their counterparts in technical schools 400 hours, in the name of getting them into the habit of work. Tellingly, even the PD-led government's ads for Fertility Day – insisting Italians ought to be making families – relied on unpaid designers.[26] No wonder 'job-givers' are getting out of the habit of paying their staff. Faced with a strike by underpaid hires, bosses at app-based food-delivery firm Foodora insisted that working there shouldn't be considered a real job but rather an 'opportunity for whoever loves getting on their bike, while also getting a little pocket money'.[27]

Road to Nowhere

There's no evidence that increased labour flexibility actually stimulates job creation – in fact, academic studies have shown the opposite.[28] The 2016 edition of the OECD's *Employment Outlook*[29] determined that making it easier to sack workers had no statistically significant effect on overall employment levels; though it drives hiring in times of economic growth, it has negative effects in times of crisis. At the same time, there is also convincing evidence that making workers' conditions more insecure actually has a negative impact on productivity growth,[30] not just by undermining workers' own commitment to their jobs but also because it increases the relative economic importance of those sectors most reliant on low-paid, low-skilled labour. Indeed, pushing down Italians' wages – with even graduates earning barely half as much as their German counterparts[31] – has encouraged firms to rely on cheap labour rather than to invest in other forms of labour saving.

Amidst a historic fall in wage and employment levels, the decline in investment has, indeed, become something of a national culture. This particularly owes to the 1990s dismantling of the Institute for National Reconstruction (IRI), a public agency long responsible for precisely the kind of strategic investment which private capitalists have proven unable to provide. As the economist Simone Gasperin's research has shown, in the 1970s, state bodies IRI and Eni represented 30 per cent of all research and development (R&D) spending (IRI was, moreover, almost twice as engaged on international markets as the Italian economy as a whole)[32]; however, its sell-off has not produced any corresponding rise in private investment. In fact, between 1995 and 2015, Italian R&D spending was only around half of French or German levels. This situation has particularly worsened thanks to the disastrous, self-defeating austerity of the post-2008 years, in which direct public investment as a whole has tumbled by some 40 per cent.

As we have seen, successive Italian prime ministers of the neoliberal centre have promised to make Italy a 'normal country', imposing liberalising reforms in the name of 'modernisation'. Yet they are instead pushing policies that restrict economic growth to what looks like a rather 'backward' form: rentiers making money off debt and asset stripping. As Marta Fana writes, the average age of machines in Italian plants – twelve years, six months – has never been higher, while since the 2008 crisis investment in fixed capital has fallen by 27 per cent.[33] Between 1981 and 1995, Italian productivity kept pace with the European average. Yet since then, in the absence of either an industrial policy or investment, the situation has been much more negative – one which appears as a dismal failure even in the Bank of Italy's own account:

> Between 1995 and 2015 manufacturing productivity grew at an average annual rate equal to 4.7 in France, 2.9 in Germany, 1.8 in Spain, and 1.2 in Italy. In the service sector, the figures are: 1.1 in France, 1.6 in Germany, 0.1 in Spain and –0.1 in Italy.[34]

Knowing the price of everything and the value of nothing, Italian elites have, indeed, spent the last three decades asset-stripping the country while running the most fundamental services into the ground. A look at the map of the nation's train networks gives us some idea what this means in reality. The state-owned Trenitalia shows that Italy can, indeed, have world-class infrastructure – the *Frecce* high-speed trains that link the main cities of northern-central Italy are clean, efficient, fast, and indeed less expensive than similar or worse services in Britain or France. But these Eurostar-style trains stand utterly at odds with what most citizens have to put up with in their everyday commutes, from the hot and over-crowded *treni regionali* that (very slowly) shuttle them around provincial Italy to the aged and fire-prone pullman services that arrive every half hour or so on the main bus routes through Rome.

The most alarming sign of Italy's crumbling infrastructure came on 14 August 2018 with the collapse of the Ponte Morandi, a motorway bridge running through the heart of Genoa. Coming just a day before the traditional *ferragosto* bank holiday, the disaster claimed some forty-three lives, from commuters to holidaymakers. At least one bucket and spade was found among the debris. The worst of a series of such incidents in recent years, the Ponte Morandi disaster also alarmingly illustrated the failures of privatisation, after three decades in which vital national infrastructure has been sold off to the highest bidder. Privatised under the centre-left D'Alema government in 1999, the concession of public motorway firm Autostrade per l'Italia has since the disaster become a byword for neglect. Later ratified in parliament by both Forza Italia and the Lega Nord, the privatisation saw massive profits drawn from tolls on badly under-maintained roads.

According to OECD data, an Italy that invested €13.66 billion in roads in 2007 cut this to just €3.39 billion in 2010 before rebounding to €5.15 billion in 2015 – still just half the levels of Germany, France, or the United Kingdom. This is to be understood as part of a general dramatic fall in public investment. The tragedy is that even as parts of Italy's infrastructure are visibly crumbling and the country struggles to recover from the crisis, meagre funds are continually channelled toward white elephant projects that serve business contractors (and in some cases, the politicians tied to them) more than they actually lead to the provision of public services. Yet, even where social movements criticise the planning of such projects, lacking a reformist perspective of their own they rarely articulate an alternative vision at the level of national politics.

Given the PD's obedience to the dogmas of budget balancing and trimmed borrowing, it is richly ironic that it should be able to claim the mantle of public investment. Yet, in the post-crisis period, *grandi opere* – the kind of infrastructure projects that might help lift Italy out of its torpor – have become a lightning rod for discontent. Epitomising this is the centrality to protest movement discourse of opposition to TAV, a high-speed rail line planned to run from Turin to Lyon. It is accused of not only disrupting the lives of communities likely to bear the impact of the line, but also of distracting attention from worthy projects. Yet visible in the opposition coming from social movements is a deeper pessimism about public investment.[35] No wonder that prominent anti-TAV campaigners have insisted that Italy is already 'excessively covered in infrastructure', or even claimed, before the Ponte Morandi collapse, that there was no need to build alternative thoroughfares.

In Italy, it is often difficult to talk about crumbling infrastructure without slipping into a hoary discourse of decadence – the once-great country no longer properly stewarded by the younger generations. It was in this key that the Ponte Morandi collapse could be presented almost as a natural disaster, reason for sadness rather than anger against those responsible.[36] When, on the first anniversary in August 2019, victims' families criticised the lack of political response – highlighting the government's failure to remove control from the private owners of Autostrade per l'Italia, as it had initially promised, Matteo Salvini chided these critics, as if their 'politicised' comments had trampled on the solemn silence owed to the dead. Indeed, despite the many failings of an Italy deprived of investment, paid work or democratic control of the economy, political responses to the crisis have rarely even raised the possibility of a renewed role for the public sector.

Italy is instead dominated by a cult of pessimism – the belief that the country's best days are behind it, and those young people who do want careers would do better to move abroad. As we shall see later, with long-standing elite corruption and failed white elephant projects, many Italians see fresh promises of infrastructure spending as only another way for politicians to line their own pockets. Even faced with low growth and decrepit road and rail lines, today's social movements are more likely to try and block new building projects than to demand fresh public investment. This does not simply identify them with the populist right – indeed, the Lega has itself long been the ally of construction magnates in its own northern heartlands. But, for this party to rise to the centre of national politics, it first had to be lifted to power by another force – one that better represented the mass disaffection of the post-crisis era. This force was the other great outsider to emerge in the era of the Second Republic – the Movimento Cinque Stelle.

4

Send in the Clowns

Thus far we have explained how the popular classes not only turned away from the old parties, but lost their political voice. The destruction of the First Republic did not enhance democratic engagement, but rather accelerated the colonisation of public life by elites whose power was rooted in other fields, from press barons to judges and technocrats. Combined with the consolidation of the Maastricht order, the effect was that the range of decisions subject to popular control narrowed at the same time as the forms of politics became more vertical and less based on mass participation. Yet, even as the focus of public debate turned away from questions of social redistribution, the material effects of political decisions were nonetheless apparent in the declining living standards of the popular classes. Already visible from the early 1990s, this narrowing of democratic and economic choice reached its culmination in the era of the 2008 crisis, as a cabinet of unelected technocrats implemented austerity measures with the support of both the main centre-left and centre-right parties. This dramatised both the crisis of representation and the social majority's feeling of powerlessness to alter their condition.

Thus far we have focused attention on the hollowing out of the Left – the transformation of the former Communist Party into a neoliberal-Europeanist force ever less anchored in the popular classes. Yet if this goes some way to explain the vacuum on this side of the political spectrum, this hardly exhausts the reasons for the rise of the populist right. Rather, the extreme volatility of Italy's party system – concerning the right as well as the left wing of politics – also owes to fragmentation within what some analysts call the 'dominant bloc'. By this they refer to the breakdown, from as early as the late 1970s, of the class-political alliances around which the prevalent institutional and economic agenda had historically been organised. In this sense, we can draw particularly useful cues from the work of the economists Bruno Amable and Stefano Palombarini.[1]

Their reading starts from the postwar existence of a dominant bloc led by the Christian Democrats, in the post–World War II period. This bloc was not reducible to the ruling classes, but rather encompassed a wider social base, uniting captains of industry with employees of the state bureaucracy, Italians reliant on state incomes, and the owners and employees of small and middle-sized businesses (SMEs). Yet in the 1980s, with the slowing of postwar growth, the advent of European monetary integration, and the turn to an economy based increasingly on debt, this last category was forced out of the dominant bloc. This was especially notable in the northeast of Italy, where SMEs integrated into German trade circuits were hit hard by rising interest rates as well as the overvaluation of the lira. While the rise of a debt-centric economy benefited financial interests and those collecting rents, this intensified splits within the dominant bloc, which was unable to cohere its fragmented interests around the European project and the politics of monetary stability. On this reading, the specifically European dimension of this turmoil meant that the voter revolt expressed in the Lega and the Movimento Cinque Stelle (Five Star Movement; M5S) emerged not in opposition to neoliberalism but on the ground of national sovereignty.[2]

These arguments usefully paint Italian neoliberalism as a part-completed revolution – a transition lacking a majoritarian social base yet transversal in its political effects, thus also shaping the ideological assumptions of 'outsider' parties. Amable and Palombarini's narrative is especially pertinent in understanding the initial rise of the Lega Nord – whose first expressions in the 1980s united regionalism with a tax-cutting opposition to the central Italian state. Yet it is also important to note that the particular forms that the call for 'sovereignty' has taken are extremely varied and far from simply defined along a national or anti-European axis. The economists' own reading highlights the endogenous, Italian-domestic economic factors behind the break-up of the old class alliance and thus reject any reading that simply focuses on constraints imposed 'from Brussels'. Yet this also poses the need to grasp the contradictory and volatile nature of the insurgent parties that have arisen since the collapse of the First Republic – apparent in the many different ideas of sovereignty and democratic control that they are built on. That is what we shall proceed to do in Chapters 4 and 5, as we study the two insurgent parties in turn – first the M5S, and then the Lega.

When these parties formed a governing coalition in June 2018, many international media were at a loss to explain such a strange hybrid.[3] This bafflement owed not least to the sense that these were rather politically diverse forces, whose breakthrough nonetheless embodied one same moment of voter revolt. Most often this took the form of projecting domestic left–right divides onto Italy: BBC *Newsnight* compared the deal to a pact between Momentum and the UK Independence Party, while centrist French press speculated on the possibility of a similar pact between left-populist Jean-Luc Mélenchon and far-right Marine le Pen. More informed analysts such as *La Stampa*'s Jacopo Iacobioni rejected this 'left-wing' characterisation of M5S, instead pointing to the Eurosceptic and conspiracy-theorist themes pushed by both parties. Yet others emphasised the obstacles that these parties had overcome in making such a pact: in the election the Lega had stood in coalition with Forza Italia, yet Berlusconi's party was the only force with which the anti-corruption M5S refused any post-election negotiations. But their choice of allies was not the only factor that threw up barriers between the insurgents. Marco Revelli suggests that they in fact embody two opposing populisms, each assembling a different kind of 'people' against the hated 'elites'. In his reading, the more southern, proletarian M5S expressed the revolt of the 'excluded', whereas the more northern, middle-class Lega represented those who had been included in the dominant bloc but now felt that their position was endangered.[4]

A closer look at the kind of Italians who voted for the M5S in March 2018 suggests that Revelli's interpretation goes some way to explaining the reality. In the 2018 election, the M5S came first or second in every region, but did particularly well in the South – its 44.4 per cent vote in the bottom half of the peninsula painted the swathe of territory from Abruzzo to Sicily in near-uniform Five Star yellow. In the First Republic era, the dominance of the Democrazia Cristiana (Christian Democracy; DC) in the South had relied on clientelist get-out-the-vote operations, based on the private appropriation of public funds. For those who saw the Italian state as a source of potential handouts, M5S's promise of welfare payments for jobseekers thus seemed like the latest iteration of an older model. But others doubted that this result should be chalked up to mere clientelism, when it so clearly expressed a thirst for political representation in parts of Italy hit hard by unemployment and mass emigration. For sociologist Domenico de Masi – at that time close to Luigi Di Maio's party – this showed that M5S had become 'the new social-democratic force in Italy – the party of the peripheries, of the unemployed, of blue-collar workers, of the South. It gathers the same social base that was once that of Berlinguer's [Italian Communist Party]'.[5]

In Amable and Palombarini's analysis, this might be taken to indicate that the M5S represents those social layers who were already outside the DC-led bloc in the First Republic – what Revelli calls the 'excluded'. Yet, even apart from the M5S's ability to win over small parts of the old *democristiano* base (SWG estimates that in 2018 it was backed by 18 per cent of former DC voters) it is also worth questioning the deeper content – the material demands, cultural values and political identity – of the voter revolt embodied by the M5S. After all, at least up to the Historic Compromise of the mid-1970s, the PCI's opposition to the dominant bloc was based not only on a specific class base, in a sociological sense, but also an alternative set of values, centred on the primacy of public good over private property. In this anti-systemic perspective, it treated such phenomena as inflation and unemployment not as incidental problems to which each government had to react, but rather as structural failings of capitalism, from which its base must be sheltered at any cost.[6] As we shall see, while the M5S is anti-establishment in its rhetoric – insisting on its difference from 'the parties' – it is not similarly anti-systemic in the sense of promoting some alternative set of values or economic priorities. Its opposition to the hegemonic order is limited to the terrain of representation – the forms of politics itself, rather than the wider organisation of society.

This is well illustrated by the personal profile of Luigi di Maio, an outsider to the political arena, who became M5S leader in 2017. Himself a southerner – a native of Pomigliano d'Arco, Naples – and just thirty-one years old at the time of the March 2018 general election, Di Maio certainly looked a lot more like the Italians on the receiving end of austerity than did the average politician. Before he became a member of parliament, he had never had a job (save a stint selling snacks at the Napoli football stadium), and he also dropped out of his degree programme. Yet Di Maio emphasised that this condition of precarity in fact extends beyond previous class divides, with all 'ordinary citizens' on the receiving end of the same situation. As he puts it, 'a worker is also a little bit of an employer, just as an employer is also a little bit of a worker'. If he attributed this line to his father – a far-right militant – this also typified the M5S bid to represent a 'transversal', post-political force, displacing the terms of political conflict away from the socioeconomic terrain to a pure question of representation. For M5S, the fundamental clash is not between classes, between North and South, or even between Italy and the European Union, but rather between the citizen and politics as a whole.

From its origin, the M5S has thus served as both a reaction against, and a radicalisation of, the popular classes' loss of their former position as a counterweight to the dominant bloc, able to assert their own distinct material demands. The period of the 2008 economic crisis, in which this democratic deficit was most manifest, provided the ideal circumstances for a revolt at the ballot box. Yet Beppe Grillo's movement built its appeal not on challenging the hegemonic economic agenda or the defence of a particular class interest, but rather the promise to remove the hierarchies built around political power itself. As the M5S founder put it in a 2013 interview with *TIME* magazine, his aim was not to become the biggest party, but rather to destroy all parties, in a 'movement' that would make 'citizens into the state'. Across over two decades of turmoil, the alternation of centre-left and centre-right had presided over an unchallengeable economic agenda, brought to its culmination by the Monti government of 2011–13. Faced with this crisis, M5S offered Italians the lever to vote out the entire political and media 'caste' – whatever the affiliation of those in power, and whatever the varied material interests of the voters themselves.

Fuck Off, PD

It's easy to find precedents for Italians' loss of faith in their political leaders – and indeed, political leaders' loss of faith in Italians. For the historically minded, 8 September evokes the infamous day in 1943 when the King and Prime Minister Pietro Badoglio fled the capital, abandoning Rome in the face of the German invasion without giving any orders to the beleaguered army. In an attempt to invoke the betrayals of more contemporary elites, in 2007 Beppe Grillo chose the anniversary of 8 September for his 'Vaffanculo Day' ('Fuck You Day'; V-Day), a series of rallies held around Italy in order to demand the cleaning up of politics. Launched through an appeal on the comedian's blog, V-Day was organised in the name of a petition to ban convicts for running for Parliament and limit MPs to a maximum two terms in office. The organisers' claimed backing for the proposed popular-initiative legislation – some 336,144 signatures – highlighted the reach of Grillo's network of support, two years after he had launched his blog beppegrillo.it.

The creation of this blog site in 2005, in collaboration with internet consultant Gianroberto Casaleggio, in fact marked something of a return from the wilderness for Grillo. After a 1986 controversy involving Prime Minister Bettino Craxi landed the comedian in hot water at public broadcaster RAI, he had made only sporadic appearances on its channels: his refusal to appear on networks associated with Silvio Berlusconi's Mediaset group or Rupert Murdoch further diminished his presence in Italians' kitchens and living rooms over the following decade. Yet as well as continuing to tour theatres around the country, around the turn of the millennium Grillo was a regular presence on street protests against Craxi's former ally Berlusconi. While at times the comedian did back initiatives driven by the radical left – for instance ecological causes or protests against Italy's involvement in the 2003 war in Iraq – the dominant message of his blog was an attack on corruption in public life and the so-called 'caste' of politicians lining their pockets, allied to a vivid denunciation of political correctness.

These movements did not impose any powerful positive agenda of their own, but rather internalised the left's loss of grand strategic visions. Under the Second Republic, the radical left instead turned to extra-institutional politics, for instance in the creation of social centres (occupied spaces, often in disused buildings), anti-redevelopment campaigns, or activism focused on alternative lifestyles. Typically built around established far-left milieus, the rise of such activities was allied to the rise of a general distrust toward Keynesian-type projects and the possibility of reforming the state, instead conceiving political action on the terrain of external resistance to the powerful. Even where parties like Rifondazione Comunista backed governments of the neoliberalised centre-left, they tended to leave the big questions of economic transformation up to more centrist forces, defensively framing their own agenda in terms of 'resistance'. Added to this were those street movements principally inspired by militant opposition to Berlusconi and critical of the institutional left for failing to combat him more effectively. Typical of this, Nanni Moretti was in the forefront of the *girotondi*, an avowedly nonpartisan movement which sought to advance 'citizen' resistance to Berlusconi, in the name of the defence of legality, the Constitution, and transparent information.

These movements were not only unable to unseat Berlusconi, but they also had no success in building lasting political structures of their own. But, as Grillo built his online presence – in what *TIME* magazine labelled one of the media sensations of 2006 – the prospect of a turn to conventional political activity began to develop. This was especially piloted through the use of the social media site MeetUp, through which dozens of local 'Friends of Beppe Grillo' groups formed. While the press quickly speculated that the comic's real aim was to create a new party, at first, he leaned toward an emphasis on 'citizen' and independent lists, which outwardly remained autonomous of his blog. Grillo abstained from the 2008 general elections, but his 'Friends' ran in both the Sicilian regional vote and Rome local contest, with percentages in the low single figures. In the June 2009 European elections, the movement made its presence more felt with its support for two candidates each elected to the Brussels parliament as independents, namely Sonia Alfano (one of the candidates it had run in the Sicilian contest) as well as anti-mafia magistrate Luigi de Magistris.

Yet this was not the limit of Grillo's ambitions. While the European elections allowed a large measure of proportional representation, affording more opportunities for smaller parties and lists, the system for domestic elections in the Second Republic had long favoured the consolidation of two rival blocs divided on left–right lines. As we have seen, this meant that even outwardly more-radical forces like Rifondazione Comunista or the Lega Nord faced a struggle between standing separately – mobilizing their own identitarian vote, but also suffering from the effect of tactical voting – or else joining a larger coalition, often at the cost of being unable to impose their specific agenda on the overall political landscape. Electoral reforms entrenching this logic thus served as a kind of glue for centre-left and centre-right coalitions, even after the disappearance of the political containers of the First Republic. It was for this reason that Grillo at first attempted to change the centre-left bloc from within, announcing that he would be running in the Democratic Party's 2009 primaries.

The PD's response to Grillo was withering, refusing point-blank to allow him to stand in its internal election. This was not unreasonable given his dubious loyalty to its cause. Indeed, the party pointed out that his recent choice to back rival candidates against it showed that, should he lose, he could hardly be expected to fall in behind whoever emerged as the winner. Yet Grillo had lost nothing from this exchange. In a now-infamous intervention, the PD's former party secretary Piero Fassino told *Repubblica TV* that 'if Grillo wants to enter politics he should set up a party and stand in elections – and we'll see how many votes he gets'.[7] This fine advice would rebound catastrophically against the PD. In truth, Grillo's sincerity in engaging with the Democrats was far from certain. But Casaleggio ruthlessly exploited this decision to communicate another message – that the establishment parties were afraid of their 'movement' and were not willing to offer left-wing voters a fair choice between Grillo and other candidates.

Grillo's nascent movement also enjoyed the support, or at least indulgence, of other public figures whose relations with the left had strained, despite their common cause against Berlusconi. Typical in this regard was the playwright Dario Fo, with his wife, Franca Rame associated with the extraparliamentary left in the 1970s and a leading defender of political prisoners. While both of them became associated with the judicial populism of the Second Republic period (Rame even ran for leader of the Italy of Values party founded by Antonio Di Pietro), it was Fo who became a prominent face of M5S, in its first general election campaign in 2013 backing both its candidates and those of Rivoluzione Civile, a front created by Rifondazione and led by anti-mafia judge Antonio Ingroia, which imitated much of Grillo's agenda. That same year, Fo published a book together with Casaleggio and Grillo in which he played the role of a sceptical left-wing convert to

M5S.[8] Another such figure, of less decidedly left-wing past, was Marco Travaglio, Italy's most famous investigative journalist and in 2009 co-founder of *Il Fatto Quotidiano*.

Il Fatto Quotidiano was never an organ of M5S, and, unlike Grillo's movement, it sought to carve out a niche in the most conventional of media – the printed press. Yet, in addition to providing relatively sympathetic coverage of M5S, it also captured something of the same anti-establishment spirit, in particular through the idea of creating a new vehicle from below that could challenge the dominant caste. Its advance stood in particular counterposition to the fate of the paper Travaglio had worked on up to that point, *l'Unità*. Founded by Antonio Gramsci in 1924, *l'Unità* had long served as the mouthpiece for the PCI and remained closely tied to its successor parties after 1991, from the PDS to the DS and the PD. Travaglio and his collaborator Peter Gomez lamented its gradual loss of critical tone even with regard to Berlusconi, in the 2005 book *L'Inciucio* (The Stitch-Up), documenting how DS leaders forced out editor Furio Colombo while refusing to move against the billionaire tycoon's own media empire. With *Il Fatto Quotidiano*, they claimed to offer a fearless reproach of the powerful, unbound by the limits of party politics.

Appearing for the first time in September 2009, *Il Fatto Quotidiano* was not, however, straightforwardly a paper of the left; it combined elements of this tradition with something more like the judicial populism of the early Clean Hands era. In this vein, it described its political line as nothing less than the 'defence of the Italian Constitution' and legality itself. The desire to vaunt its independence was moreover displayed in its funding. The Italian press has long been dominated by either direct political patronage – as in the case of *Il Giornale*, run by Berlusconi's brother Paolo, or *l'Unità*'s links to the PCI and its successors – or alignment with other corporate interests, for instance the historic ownership of Rome daily *Il Messaggero* by the Montedison energy group. Yet most papers also heavily rely on state funding, widely perceived as blunting their critical edge. First created by a crowdfunding campaign, *Il Fatto Quotidiano* promised to do without this institutional support – though its leading voice Travaglio would also make regular appearances on the La7 TV station run by the Cairo Communication group.

The early M5S took an even more absolutist position against the established media, insisting that Italy did not need journalists at all. This was particularly notable in the most energetic phase of Grillo's activity, in the run-up to the 2013 general election, including a national tour. Preferring to address his followers directly (and without challenge) via the beppegrillo.it blog as well as his town-square rallies, Grillo forbade M5S figures from speaking to journalists or from appearing on television. At the same time as refusing to participate in the 'media game', presented as a means of catching out M5S members rather than taking their ideas seriously, Grillo's movement called not for the empowerment of critical media but rather a general destruction of the press 'caste'. In a 2013 interview with *TIME* magazine, Grillo insisted that the 'three [biggest] papers and seven TV channels' forming public opinion were 'worse than the parties' and 'part of the system'.[9] He called for the removal of all state subsidies for newspapers as well as the selling off of public broadcaster RAI.

Such displays of differentness, as well as the apparent democracy of the town-square rally, appealed to Italians' sense that they had been deprived of political choice. A simple message of 'bringing honesty back into fashion' insisted that removing forms of intermediation like parties and the press could allow citizens directly to speak for themselves, without institutional filters. Yet Grillo also offered his own form of mediation. Despite his aggressive attacks on journalists, deemed mere mouthpieces for 'the system', Grillo congratulated himself for having turned popular anger in a peaceful direction: as he put it in this same *TIME* interview, 'I channel all this rage into this movement of people, who then go and govern. They should be thanking us one by one. If we fail, [Italy] is headed for violence in the streets'.[10] His favoured tactic for channelling anger, however, also involved harsh trolling of the existing political codes – for instance, raising the call to 'march on Rome' (an obvious reference to Mussolini) or staging a filmed meeting with leaders of neofascist social centre CasaPound in order to provoke establishment disgust and thus reinforce his message of differentness.[11]

Grillo's war on political mediation extended beyond pro-austerity parties to target organised labour itself. Of course, his references to the main party of the centre-left – the 'PD without an L', a cutting reference to its similarities to Silvio Berlusconi's Popolo della Libertà, PdL) – sought to exploit disillusionment at its failure to stand up for its own base. Yet, at the same time, Grillo also sharply denounced rival forms of popular mobilisation. While M5S commented favourably on amorphous or apparently 'leaderless' social movements, far different were its attitudes toward the deeper-rooted structures of organised labour. This was most infamously symbolised by a Grillo speech in Brindisi, broadcast live on his blog – part of his national tour before the 2013 general election – where he called for 'a state with balls' to 'eliminate the trade unions', declaring that there was 'no need' for what were now an 'old structure like the parties'.[12] Coming soon after the CasaPound meeting, unions responded by asking what kind of 'democracy' the M5S leader was really looking for.

A response not only to post-2008 austerity but a quarter century of political and economic volatility, M5S never adopted the message of left-populist parties such as Podemos in Spain or Syriza in Greece, promising a break with neoliberalism. While these forces similarly claimed to assert citizen power against the existing party duopoly, they were especially driven by the anti-austerity movements of 2011, which had seen the large-scale occupation of public squares as well as a rise in strike activity. Even when Pablo Iglesias's Podemos vaunted its claim to stand beyond left and right, this was mainly conceived as a way of distancing itself from the more established centre-left PSOE,[13] and both the personal biography of its leaders (rooted in the Communist Party) and its concrete proposals unambiguously stood in the traditions of labour and social protection. Syriza was even more conventionally left-wing, though in the early 2010s it also swallowed up sections of the once-dominant centre-left (PASOK), whose enforcement of austerity measures (and coalition with the centre-right New Democracy) unravelled both its patronage structures and its historic ties to labour.

Quite different was the Italian case. Mario Monti's administration clearly played into the hands of M5S's argument that politics had grown apart from citizen control, given both the manner of its formation (as a deal lined up by the president under the pressure of the bond markets and ECB) and its parliamentary basis (backed by both main parties).

The M5S not only carried forth a message of direct democracy but had also emerged outside of existing parliamentary parties, and thus appeared in outright counterposition to this form of politics. Yet, whereas left-wing parties in other southern European countries sought to link the crisis of representation to attacks on popular living standards, in Italy it was instead the narrative of the recent decades of judicial populism that reaffirmed itself, as the M5S counterposed the 'lying, corrupt politicians' to the 'honest' ordinary citizen. It seemed that after a quarter century of economic stagnation and privatizations, most Italians saw post-2008 austerity measures with a sense of grim inevitability, rather than as something which a different government might reverse. Indeed, revealing its own anti-political mores, M5S's hostility was far more directed against 'the parties' (and especially the PD) than the Monti cabinet itself.

This also informed the communication strategy which M5S directed against the Monti government in its first years, focused on preparing for its first general election test rather than any immediate efforts to resist austerity. Despite its connection to local protests against infrastructure projects, M5S was not an organised presence within the most conventional anti-austerity mobilisations of this period, such as the 'No Monti Day' called by left-wing parties and trade unions on 27 October 2012. Rather, the constant narrative put forward by Grillo's party was the call 'Kick them all out!', the redemptive electoral moment in which Italians would simply be able to vote out the hated 'caste'. This was a message which the M5S leader broadcast in his so-called Tsunami Tour of January–February 2013. While policy detail – or even a general orientation – remained slight, Grillo boasted that 'nothing will be as before', that the 'old world is over', that the TV and media were the 'Wall of Jericho in defence of the indefensible', that the stock exchange and bond markets were 'subject to manipulation', and that the campaign might be 'the thirty-nine days that shake Italy'.[14]

Yet, while Grillo attacked out-of-touch politicians for failing to recognise popular suffering, his project did not itself seek to empower the disenfranchised – or even unite them around common material interests. In their book discussion with Fo, he and Casaleggio instead advanced a hodgepodge of complaints, from the sell-off of Italian state assets to the aggravation of the crisis by 'thieving politicians' and the dangers of the rise of the far right. A notable theme of Grillo's message was his condemnation of so-called 'protected' categories – those who were not suffering like their fellow Italians. This was visible even after the party's electoral breakthrough, which came with the general election of 25 February 2013. In a blog post, the day after a contest where the M5S had scored strongly among young voters but under 10 per cent among pensioners, he divided Italians into 'group A', the young, unemployed, and precarious, who had lost hope, and 'group B', happy to keep things just as they were.[15] He spoke of the 'unsustainable weight of the state paying 19 million pensions and 4 million wages a month . . . an infernal machine that needs replacing with a citizens' income'. As he put it in a web-radio interview on 29 March, a 'good part of these [pensioners and employees] were barely touched by the crisis'.[16] His citizens' income proposed to pay them €600 a month.

This lack of a clear social agenda was combined with the strongly contradictory positions that M5S expressed with regard to the European integration process, venting anti-Brussels sentiments and criticisms of the single currency while remaining more circumspect in terms of policy prescriptions. The radical *tone* of Grillo's communications was often married to a tepid promise of actual changes, it being assumed that the European architecture was both unreformable and here to stay. Typical of this was a rally at Turin's Piazza Castello in the run-up to the 2014 European election: Beppe Grillo framed his call for a break with the Fiscal Compact in vulgar terms, describing Matteo Renzi as a 'moron' who 'licked Merkel's big German arse'; putting the same message in more polite terms, in an interview for *Il Fatto Quotidiano* Gianroberto Casaleggio described the political project for a united Europe as 'lost' but insisted that he wanted to make the euro work properly. Asked by Peter Gomez and his colleague 'if the critics of the euro are saying Italy's crisis does not depend on [its own] corruption, bureaucracy, waste and tax evasion', Casaleggio insisted that Italy did, indeed, need to cut spending:

> The euro and Europe can't be an alibi. Today we spend €800bn. Of this €100bn is interest on debt. Of the other €700bn, we could cut €200bn. I'll discuss with Europe how it's managed, but that doesn't excuse me of getting my own house in order.[17]

M5S leaders thus both denounced the external constraints while also accepting that public spending did need cutting.

Such contradictory statements typified the difficulties in pinning down the M5S within a left–right spectrum or indeed on the axis of Europeanism and sovereigntism. Yet this was, in fact, part of its identity – and its appeal. It can be distorting to judge a party in terms of its hidden intentions rather than what it openly says to its electorate. What M5S did was to express popular anger at perceived injustices and undeserved concentrations of wealth and power, while keeping its own proposed policy measures both vague and decidedly unambitious. M5S did freely denounce a host of institutions, from banks to ('current') European Union rules, political parties, trade unions, and media. Yet, at the same time, it could maintain its own unity precisely with a rhetorical focus on its own nonpolitical character. This allowed it continually to centre its concrete proposals on the terrain of representation and public morality, whether limiting representatives to two terms in office, promising to break up media monopolies, or calling for an end to politicians' protections from prosecution.

A PD without an L

The results of the February 2013 general election were an earthquake. Having never previously stood in such a national-level contest, M5S immediately vaulted to first place. It was not the largest coalition; that honour instead went to the centre-left bloc led by Pier Luigi Bersani. Yet the ex-Communist PD leader fell short of expectations, his 10 million votes only slightly beating a surprisingly resurgent Berlusconi (9.9 million) and M5S (which itself took 8.7 million votes). While Bersani and his allies had won an absolute majority in the Chamber of Deputies – the Porcellum[18] electoral law guaranteed the largest coalition 340 of the 630 seats – this same mechanism failed to operate as planned in the Senate, when the bonus was instead distributed on a regional basis. The effect of the tri-cornered result was parliamentary deadlock, with the centre-left only taking 123 of the 315 seats in the Senate (with 158 needed for a majority), as opposed to 117 for the centre-right and 54 for the M5S. Grillo's movement was in no position to take charge of Italy – rather, its success was precisely that it had prevented any other bloc from being able to govern alone.

As coalition talks loomed, Grillo emphasised the need for transparency, insisting that any negotiations would have to be livestreamed online. Yet rather more difficult to control was the decision on the next president of the republic. In the Italian system, this figure does not lead the day-to-day operations of government, instead serving as a guarantor of constitutional propriety; he is directly elected by parliamentarians, not the public. Yet the fact that this vote took place in the immediate post-election period invariably made it into a proxy for the contest over coalition formation. M5S put forward the name of Stefano Rodotà, a jurist and former PDS man, in the outward interest of building bridges with the centre-left. However, after their alliance in backing the Monti cabinet since September 2011, the PD's own legislators instead tilted toward a coalition with Berlusconi. The PD leader Bersani first put forward the name of Catholic trade union leader Franco Marini, but faced with opposition from Florence mayor Matteo Renzi he instead backed former premier Romano Prodi, himself of Christian-Democratic background. While the centre-left parties agreed on Prodi, when the secret ballot took place the actual number of votes was far short of what it should have been – indicating that Bersani was losing control over his own MPs and senators. Eventually, Napolitano was asked to stay on as head of state, indeed as the first-ever president to begin a second term. On 24 April he appointed the PD's Enrico Letta to form a government of national unity, including Berlusconi's party.

The sense of a stitch-up animated fresh complaints by

Grillo, who cried 'coup'. Doubtless, it was unedifying to see Napolitano wheeled out to bring together another such pact, not least the manner in which he christened the unity of centre-left and centre-right. The following day, in a speech at the former SS prison at Via Tasso – marking the anniversary of Italy's liberation from fascism – he compared the demands of forming a grand coalition with the 'courage, firmness and sense of unity decisive to the victory of the Resistance'. Grillo angrily shot back – insisting that the partisans' legacy had 'died with the appointment of a Bilderberg group member as prime minister'.[19] But the real power-play was by Renzi, the thirty-eight-year-old now pushing himself to the centre of internal PD affairs. With Bersani ejected from the party-secretary job, and Berlusconi almost immediately felled by a fraud conviction, the liberal Renzi was well primed to push himself to the centre of Italian politics. His mandate came in a subsequent primary, which saw him elected by 68 per cent of PD supporters. By the start of 2014 he had begun to assert his own claim to the prime minister's job.

Letta's coalition marked a first for the PD; having long sought the pacts with centrists that could keep out the ogrish Berlusconi, in April 2013 it directly joined with him in government. For the left-wing critics of the PD this was not entirely surprising, given both the recent pact under Monti and the party's previous failure to tackle Berlusconi's business interests head-on. Yet this embrace did not last for long. Berlusconi's troubles with the courts had begun to pile up, and in August he was finally convicted on fraud charges – the first time that he had exhausted all his appeals for any particular case. The media tycoon did not suffer too much from 200 hours of community service: he spent it as an entertainer in care homes, reprising his youthful career as a crooner on cruise ships. The problem lay rather more in its effect on his political ambitions. For two decades, he had managed his own party without challenge, selecting candidates, ministers and allies to his heart's content. But with Popolo della Libertà now a junior partner in government with the PD, fissure lines opened up in the party. The trigger came when the government refused to shield him from his conviction – thus ensuring he would be banned from public office. He quit the coalition – but none of his ministers followed him.

The breakdown of Berlusconi's authority heralded wider realignments on the right – and a fight to conquer the political space hitherto occupied by Popolo della Libertà. Whereas the tycoon rekindled his old Forza Italia party, whose banners continued to proclaim him its candidate for prime minister, Interior Minister Angelino Alfano – a long-time Berlusconi protégé – instead declared the creation of a new force that would soldier on in partnership with the PD, Nuovo Centrodestra (New Centre-Right, NCD). But with the natural centre of gravity on the centre-right now thrown into crisis, an opportunity also opened up for forces further to the right, outside government. These were, however, themselves at an early stage of reorganisation. Created at the end of 2012, Giorgia Meloni's new postfascist party Fratelli d'Italia united old hands of the MSI like Alemanno and former defence minister Ignazio La Russa, but it polled only 2 per cent in the 2013 general election. The apparently more dynamic force was the Lega. While it had been reduced to just 4 per cent in the election, it had held on to its northern heartlands and rallied behind a new leader – Matteo Salvini.

Yet not only right-wingers hoped to exploit the crisis of Berlusconism. For the PD leader Matteo Renzi, elected secretary on 8 December 2013, the hope was that his party could scoop up the centrist fragments of Popolo della Libertà, building a broad-tent centrist force. This also served as a means of rhetorically distancing himself from the PD's left-wing origins, or even its social-democratic identity, as he instead called for the creation of a 'party of the nation'. Ironically, this first took the form of a bid to close down the political space for his own coalition allies, through the mechanism of an electoral reform that would marginalise small centrist forces like Alfano's NCD. On 5 December, the Constitutional Court had declared the existing electoral law partly unconstitutional, and on 2 January 2014 Renzi thus issued a call for a new system that would weaken the senate and restore an exchange of power between two major blocs. The M5S cried foul, but Berlusconi agreed to the initiative – and talks with Renzi at the PD's Via Nazareno headquarters. The negotiations restored Berlusconi some of his institutional legitimacy, moreover allowing Renzi to marginalise prime minister Letta. In February, Renzi finally used his power to oust Letta from office – installing himself as prime minister on 22 February.

With European elections scheduled for May, Renzi also sought a personal mandate. His aim in this election was both to unite the centre, scooping up fragments of Forza Italia, while also recapturing the political initiative from M5S. In particular, while the PD had failed to ram home a general election victory in either 2008 or 2013, this contest provided an opportunity to show that it could push back against the rising 'outsider' parties. In this cause, Renzi made a populist offer of his own. From the beginning of his term he presented himself as the 'demolition man' crusading against old elites, and in this election also advanced retail policies such as an

€80 a month tax relief for all families. The result was a huge mandate, winning some 11.2 million votes – over 41 per cent of the total. This placed the PD far ahead of the 5.8 million score for M5S and the 4.6 million for Forza Italia – illustrating its crisis, this latter party had lost over 6 million votes compared to the previous European election in 2009. Salvini's Lega recovered slightly compared to February 2013's general election disaster, taking almost 1.7 million votes nationally. Its 6 per cent of the vote was in fact a sharp decrease on its previous European election outing, but nonetheless showed that it was able to withstand Bossi's departure.

From the start of his government, Renzi's populist interventions were more a matter of his political style than the substance of his policy offer. The €80 tax break he offered in the 2014 European contest was in fact a rare instance of concrete aid to working families. Rather more important to his appeal was the carefully cultivated image of a premier who wore open-necked shirts or spoke directly into the parliamentary cameras, indeed speaking over the heads of legislators to simulate 'eye contact' with TV viewers.[20] All this provided a means by which the career politician could vaunt a folksy, no-bullshit image. In the bid for centrist votes, the 'demolition man' persona was allied to a confrontation with his own base, indeed mounting free-marketeer reforms that even Berlusconi would have balked at. The removal of Article 18 of the Workers' Statute (thus allowing employers to sack staff at will), the Good School reform (making educators' employment status more precarious), and the introduction of *l'alternanza scuola-lavoro* (compulsory unpaid internships for high-school students) all set the PD on the war-path against the unions on whose support it had once relied.

In his early moment of hubris, Renzi liked to compare himself with a past rock star of the neoliberalised centre-left, Tony Blair. As in many attempts to invoke foreign 'models' in Italian politics, this reference point was, however, curiously parochial, the PD leader seemingly having remained oblivious to Blair's growing unpopularity in his own country or even the reasons for his initial success.[21] The injection of English-language slogans into Renzi's discourse was not entirely new – in the PD's first general election campaign in 2008, leader Walter Veltroni had incautiously copied Barack Obama's slogan 'Yes We Can', in a transparent bid to capture some political stardust. If this recourse to a foreign vocabulary in the name of seeming 'modern' perhaps fed a sense of the PD's elitism – and exposed some rather dodgy pronunciation – rather more damaging was its deeper failure to learn the lessons of New Labour. For while Renzi's bid for the centre ground did temporarily allow him to mop up Forza Italia votes, he also radicalised the split with his party's former labour-movement base.

We have already seen the process that took the PD to adopt liberal-centrist positions. Yet post-crisis conditions harshened its attacks on workers' rights. Back in the 1990s, New Labour had aggressively promoted middle-class values of aspiration and business success but maintained a residual attachment to trade unions and historic Labour achievements, for instance increasing investment in the National Health Service even while introducing private contractors. This allowed it to buy off parts of its base even while shifting to a more 'pro-business' agenda. Renzi's confrontation with his base was far more one-sided, pushing previous centre-left governments' privatising agenda into a far-reaching assault on both employment rights and the unions' bargaining position. The Italian General Confederation of Labour (CGIL), historically led by the scions of the PCI, had remained aligned to the PDS and its successors over the 1990s and 2000s, embracing the idea of 'social partnership'. Renzi, however, high-handedly dismissed this alliance, forcing CGIL leader Susanna Camusso to break with the PD.

Renzi's attempt to revolutionise the PD also fuelled the attacks coming from his most dangerous rival – the M5S. The split within Berlusconi's PdL had seen this particular acronym removed from the political arithmetic. However, the M5S's attacks on the 'PD without an L' were unabated and received fresh fuel from events in the capital. Again, the central issue was the takeover of the political system by corruption. December 2014 saw a wave of arrests across Rome, exposing the existence of a criminal organisation soon labelled 'Mafia Capitale'. Its turnover was estimated at over €90 million a year, the extension of its business networks owing to the contracts it won by bribing politicians across the centre-left and centre-right divide. Photos of the collaborators dining together drove home the M5S message of a corrupt caste united in their shady dealings.

The revelations struck a devastating blow to the established parties in the council. Mafia Capitale's ties with city hall – through which criminal gangs took control of state tenders for services ranging from road repair to the management of migrant reception – had principally run through former Movimento Sociale Italiano (Italian Social Movement) man Gianni Alemanno, from 2008 to 2013 the mayor of Rome. Despite his integration into the mainstream centre-right, he remained tied to figures like Massimo Carminati, a terrorist from the 1970s fascist group Armed Revolutionary

Nuclei. Carminati ally Salvatore Buzzi, the Forza Italia group leader in the Lazio regional council, was at the centre of the Mafia Capitale network. Yet it also included two leading lights in the PD, namely Luca Odevaine (deputy chief of staff for former PD leader Walter Veltroni during his early 2000s spell as mayor of Rome) and Mirko Coratti, PD president of Rome city council. Both were arrested in June 2015 and ultimately sentenced to long prison terms.

The scandal perfectly played into M5S's hands – and Renzi's reaction made things even worse for the local PD. The mayor of Rome from June 2013, PD man Ignazio Marino was himself without blame in the affair. Indeed, he had been actively involved in exposing it. In June 2014, after he had been approached by the Mafia Capitale group, Marino presented the incriminating evidence to police, in an effort to suppress the rampant criminality within the city council. This was not, however, enough to put Marino on the right side of the 'anti-corruption' campaign driven by local press as well as the M5S. This latter party instead whipped up a scandal around the mayor himself, designed to highlight his supposed hypocrisy in condemning his corrupt predecessor. The trivial brouhaha directed against the soft-left mayor was notably illustrated by 'Panda gate', in which it was revealed that Marino had failed to pay his parking fines – an offense magnified in newspaper reports by the insistence that the nerdish former transplant surgeon looked ridiculous driving a Fiat Panda. Other offenses, similarly held up as an illustration of the opulence of the 'caste', included Marino's use of his official credit card to pay for a €55 bottle of wine in a restaurant.

No one – including Marino's own PD 'colleague' Renzi – seemed to care that this recently elected mayor had tried to root out real criminality by violent gangs and that this kind of corruption – costing taxpayers hundreds of millions of euros – far outweighed his own more minor indiscretions. The Mafia Capitale scandal had fed the mantra that the parties were 'all the same' and that Marino was himself incompetent, not least because he drove a ridiculous car. This gaffe-prone reputation worsened after a further incident in which Marino followed Pope Francis around on a tour of Philadelphia – the pontiff disdainfully told press that he had not invited the Rome mayor to come with him.[22] From the national government, Renzi chose to stick the knife in, airily speculating in national press that the Roman mayor should consider his future; as Interior Minister Angelino Alfano decided whether to take the capital's governance under direct control, the PD group in Rome itself voted to toss Marino aside. The mayor was disgusted by being forced to back down and, after having initially resigned, made a brief attempt to reclaim his position. The result was a temporary administration in the capital and early elections.

The tedious to-and-fro of the corruption allegations (joined with threatened, but never tested, libel charges among the main protagonists), however, intersected with underlying grievances that fuelled the mood of revolt against the PD. Not least of these was the disastrous state of rubbish collection in the capital, a sign of municipal incompetence able to offend multiple senses at once. Yet the real lightning rod for the voter revolt was immigration. The scandal had struck during a phase in which migrant numbers were rapidly rising across Europe, especially due to the Syrian civil war and conflicts in sub-Saharan Africa. One of the services contracted out to Mafiosi had involved the hosting of asylum seekers, with the €35 a day payment per migrant (often misrepresented as a payment *to* the migrants themselves). For M5S, this was a lightning-rod issue: an example of the profligacy of politicians willing to pour funds into a 'migrant business' at taxpayers' expense.

The politics of anti-corruption, and the visceral condemnation of aloof elites, had combined with the even more emotive theme of immigration and national identity. This would also mark M5S's campaign for the June 2016 mayoral contest, in which its candidate was the twenty-seven-year-old Virginia Raggi. Having trained as a lawyer, she had worked for the firm of Berlusconi's former defence minister Cesare Previti, himself banned from public office in 2007 after a corruption conviction. Given the setbacks for the previous administration and indeed the infighting within the PD camp, Raggi's victory was, from the outset, close to assured. Her positions showed M5S's attempt to both ride the anti-immigration mood and appeal to former left-wing voters. A call for the registration of Roma people was thus posed both as a means of liberating them from their marginal condition and lack of access to social services, and as a necessary security measure never taken by 'the parties' immersed in the 'immigration business'.

This was also a moment in which the overlap of the themes raised by the M5S and the Lega became more sharply apparent. In March 2015 leading M5S activist Alessandro di Battista issued a video on social media promising to 'dismantle the Lega in 5 minutes',[23] denouncing the hard-right party's claim to represent a truly 'anti-*casta*' force when so many of its local representatives were lining their pockets at taxpayers' expense through dubious spending claims. He began the video citing messages from supporters asking that he call out the Lega's racism, but insisted that it was more effective to confront them on the use of public funds, as he then proceeded to do. Yet both parties were beginning to fuse 'anti-corruption' politics with a denunciation of mass immigration. While M5S maintained a generic defence of the right to asylum, its call to 'stop the immigration business' (citing one Mafia Capitale conspirator to the effect that 'migration is worth more money than drugs') increasingly became the framing device for its response to the migrant crisis.

In this sense, the June 2016 result in Rome expressed the collapse of the PD's historic social base, a phenomenon greatly aggravated in the period of the economic crisis. This was especially clear in the second round of the contest, in which Raggi faced off against the PD candidate Roberto Giachetti. Maps of the results showed only the very smartest central neighbourhoods in PD red – once the colour of the workers' movement – whereas the old proletarian neighbourhoods as well as the city periphery were a sea of M5S yellow. Yet if this working-class revolt was fuelled by material difficulties, Raggi's campaign brought it together with a generalised rejection of the PD. Winning over two-thirds of the vote, the young lawyer could quite genuinely claim to stand above political divides, as she rallied the support of Salvini and other far-right enemies of the PD as well as former communists hostile to the party's neoliberal turn. It seemed that Raggi's campaign had operated as an empty signifier – an almost blank screen onto which different groups could project their discontent. Yet the more opaque structures within her party machine would ensure that the participants in the anti-caste revolt would have little actual control over M5S itself.

Directed Democracy

Indeed, the year 2016 would also provide the second great example of M5S's ambiguity. Having lost Rome in June, Renzi tried to recapture the mood of discontent, himself making a fresh promise to cut the cost of politics. Claiming that his plans to 'liberalise' the economy were being held back by entrenched elites – from parliament to provincial administrators and the trade unions – Renzi called a referendum for December that would push Italy toward a more executive-centric model. He sought to do away with both its perfect bicameralism (that is, the Senate's ability to initiate legislation on an equal footing to the Chamber of Deputies) and the powers enjoyed by the provinces. Posing as a maverick leader who stood above his own party, Renzi portrayed reform as a way in which voters could punish 'the politicians'. To this end, he adopted crass slogans calling on voters to 'take away the armchairs' so beloved of his fellow legislators. However, overconfident in his own providential role, Renzi also personalised the vote, insisting that he would resign if the reform did not pass.

This proved strongly counterproductive, for as with the M5S campaign in the Rome contest, it ensured that very different forms of opposition and discontent with the PD could combine. The speculation on Renzi's own future, and even the possibility that a No vote would spark an early general election, meant that the specific measures of the constitutional reform bore an only secondary influence on the 4 December 2016 vote. If its real contents mattered to anyone, this was most of all on the left wing of Italian politics – the National Italian Partisans' Association (ANPI) condemned the attacks on the Constitution born of the

Resistance. Opponents of Renzi within the PD like former premier Massimo d'Alema also took sides against the reform, perhaps with more than an eye on ridding themselves of the prime minister. The right-wing parties, which had themselves proposed a similar reform in 2006, also called for a No vote in the name of ousting Renzi. But, without doubt, the biggest force in stopping the reform was the M5S. Its campaign was narrowly focused on immediate political consequences, highlighting the prospect that a No vote could bring the early downfall of Renzi and thus the early elections that would sweep the M5S itself into national level office. When the results came in, some 59 per cent of voters had opted for No – and the insurgent M5S could once again claim victory.

For the prime minister's allies, even this defeat showed that he was a 'winner'. Having already received a 'plebiscite' of support in the European elections of 2014, Renzi had again rallied 41 per cent of Italians behind his project. Yet as promised, his referendum setback led immediately to his resignation, replaced as prime minister by PD colleague Paolo Gentiloni. But the nearly 20 million votes against his Constitution combined all manner of forms of dissent. Particularly notable was the youth vote – a massive 70 per cent of twenty-five-to-thirty-four-year-olds rejected the change.[24] If Renzi's measures promised to slash the number of parliamentarians and allow the government greater freedom to combat establishment 'conservatism', in fact it was the oldest Italians who backed the planned reforms. It seemed that the specific proposals made by Renzi, from weakening the power of the Senate to abolishing the provinces, were rather less important than the ability to vote against the prime minister himself. And the M5S, which itself backed the slimming of the central state just as Renzi had proposed, was in the forefront of the campaign to leave the Constitution just the same.

Yet, if M5S call for a No vote had a strong opportunistic streak, this also typified its ambiguous relationship to republican institutions – and to democracy itself. From the outset, M5S had bluntly affirmed its separateness from 'politics' and 'parties' in general, instead identifying as a pure expression of the Italian population. Its crude moral binaries – 'honest citizens' standing up to the unaccountable political 'caste' – were amplified by its exaltation of the internet as a democratic alternative to mass media controlled by the likes of Berlusconi, Murdoch, or indeed RAI, a public broadcaster which is managed by party appointees. Where Grillo had found himself edged out from the mass media, as M5S leader he turned this relationship on its head, as he instead imposed his own limits on what mass media could do. Banning his movement's representatives from appearing on TV, Grillo instead forced them to release public statements only through his own personal blog – thus skirting media questioning.

Grillo's messaging strategy especially relied on his collaboration with web entrepreneur Casaleggio. He could, with good reason, term himself Grillo's 'guru', as he hitched his own marketing strategies to the comic's public face. He had begun his career working for typewriter kingpin Adriano Olivetti, himself author of several political texts that advocated the overcoming of the clash between labour and capital via the rule of enlightened administrators who could run the economy in the general interest. Yet what Casaleggio took from his mentor was less Olivetti's utopian desire for social harmony than his post-democratic conclusions. His interventions were strongly imbued with the notion that the expert command of transparent information –

monitoring inputs and production levels and canvassing popular sentiment on an ongoing basis – could replace mass political decision-making and the processes of democratic competition.

As an employee of British web consultant WebEgg, in the 1990s Casaleggio had taken a particular interest in the use of online tools to manipulate public opinion. In his acidic deconstructions of M5S's self-promotion, Jacopo Iacoboni has exposed the breathtaking cynicism of Casaleggio's thinking, explicitly laid out in early experiments for hijacking discussions on web forums. He cites former WebEgg employee Carlo Baffè, who explains how Casaleggio coached his staff in 'using forums to pass off certain positions of Roberto's as if they were the fruit of democratic discussions'. 'One Intranet member would launch the discussion on a theme, another would respond with a contrary position, then two others took the side of the first . . . creating what Roberto called the "avalanche of agreement" '. But, as Baffè understood, 'At first this was a fun game . . . but I later realised that this was nothing but an experiment in social engineering to understand the most effective methods for manipulating opinion and creating consent with an apparently democratic discussion'.[25]

Iacoboni highlights the eclectic views that Casaleggio derived from his engagement with Olivetti (and indeed, attendance at Bossi rallies). These politics included certain far-right themes but above all centred on conspiracist thinking and globalist plots. This outlook was notably expressed in his 2008 video *Gaia*.[26] Outlining a single organic worldview, the seven-minute film purported to predict the state at which humanity would arrive in 2054, an online community of 'world citizens' devoid of conflict. As the viewer able to withstand the voice-over will appreciate, this video brought together a ragbag of theories about the control of information; the sway of Masonic, religious, and financial bodies; and the elite meetings at Bilderberg. Following in a long tradition of theories designed to appeal to the alienated and atomised, the world's injustices were blamed not on fundamental power structures but on 'corruption'; further lightening the load on viewers, the imagined future order would owe not to social mobilisation but to apocalyptic redemption, thanks to a World War III mooted for the 2020s.

Gaia offered no brilliant insights into the contemporary condition but did express the conception of politics that spread among M5S's noisier supporters. The fall of the old mass parties, the judicialisation of politics and Berlusconian dominance all nourished Casaleggio's narrative, as alienated citizens unable to make meaningful political decisions looked up powerless at the distant and personalised elites. With social media on their side, M5S's organisation instead claimed to stand on the democracy of the internet – 'uno vale uno' – anyone's say should count as much as anyone else's. Ironically, however, precisely what M5S offered was mediation, since its fans would not intervene politically themselves, as in the form of party militants, but rather cheerlead online for their supposed champions. A student of polling techniques and focus groups since the dawn of the internet, Casaleggio knew from his experience running Usenet forums that he could get the right answer as long as he asked his followers the right question – especially if his sock puppets were themselves active in the conversation.

In this schema, the Grillo-Casaleggio duo were every bit as much political entrepreneurs as Berlusconi, with the key generational difference that they replaced the more obviously passive TV viewer with the online fan. While the billionaire tycoon entered politics in 1994 in order to defend his preexisting media empire, M5S leaders' success instead lay in using a political vehicle to build a lucrative online presence. In fact, much like the Rousseau platform – the means by which M5S supporters took part in online votes, on such questions as the selection of candidates and the ranking of programmatic pledges – Grillo's blog belonged to Casaleggio Associates, harvesting the revenue from what had by 2007 become one of the world's most-visited websites. This moreover allowed M5S's leaders to maintain total control of its internal processes. The fact that Rousseau was private property (and that the business party had no formal membership structures) simply allowed any discordant voices to be deleted as soon as they began to make trouble, ensuring its proprietors' iron control over its internal processes – like a more heavily censored version of Facebook or Twitter.

Moreover, a sharp division of authority within the movement allowed its structures to be defended from the actions of its ephemeral leaders and representatives. Particularly key to this constellation was the role of Grillo himself. Given his 1985 manslaughter conviction (owing to a road accident), he fell foul of M5S's call for convicts to be barred from public office, so instead took up a place as the 'guarantor' of its internal constitution, buttressed by the authority drawn from his role in its foundation. Given the generally fideistic attitude toward Grillo among the M5S's own fan base, this allowed him to perform something a little like the role of a constitutional monarch, standing for the prestige of its institutions while not letting them be sullied by the comings and goings of everyday politics. Where the Queen's place guarantees her ownership of England's swans, the M5S *garante* would instead draw his particular reward in Google Ads revenue. *Bloomberg* noted the remarkable invention of 'politics for profit',[27] through means barely less transparent than Berlusconi's own.

M5S rapidly became known for its control-freakery, including in its relations with its elected officials. The conception of its representatives as delegates rather than elected individuals set the tone for a disciplinarian approach that silenced all traces of internal dissension. That began in September 2012 when Emilia-Romagna regional councillor Giovanni Favia (one of the M5S's first elected officials) was expelled for criticising Casaleggio on TV.[28] One MP, Massimo Artini, was kicked out simply for setting up a listserv among M5S representatives not hosted by Casaleggio himself.[29] So many were the expulsions that after its first five years in parliament the M5S was 21 MPs and 19 senators poorer than at the start – a quarter of all its representatives. In order to maintain this image of unanimity, M5S members typically abstained on contentious proposals, precisely in order to maintain the image of a 'blank screen' onto which almost any form of discontent could be projected. Exemplary was a vote on gay adoption, promoted by Matteo Renzi's Democratic administration, in which M5S MPs refrained from voting, but then gave opposite reasons for doing so, whether invoking Catholic family values or claiming the bill did not go far enough.

As we shall see in Chapter 5, this approach came unstuck in the M5S's period in government, as alliance with the far-stronger-defined Lega compelled it more clearly to define its political positions, or at least drove contradictions within its ranks. For now, we might note that, in the period of Luigi Di

Maio's leadership, there has been a general tendency for M5S to abandon the trappings of differentness, as its own representatives' record in office – together with the fading of its initial sense of novelty – has undermined its binary of honest citizens and corrupt politicians. Having left behind its purely oppositional role, it has moved to abandon the two-term limit on elected officials – after all, now M5S's own MPs are now on their second spell in Parliament. It has done away with the charter expelling all officials who come under judicial investigation – for some of M5S's own have faced police scrutiny. And it has done away with the ban on appearing on TV – for now in government, M5S can dictate to journalists the terms on which they will be interviewed.

5

Salvini's Triumph

Lampedusa is in Africa. More importantly, it is in the European Union. The tiny Italian island in the southern Mediterranean has become a landing point for desperate souls crossing from Libya and Tunisia, the luckiest of whom make it there alive. If such a setting may seem as far as imaginable from the kind of Italy the Lega has long represented, its repurposing as a processing site for migrants has turned its politics upside down. In the European elections in May 2019, the Lega scored some 45.9 per cent in this southernmost of Italian territories, albeit on a rock-bottom 26.6 per cent turnout. Lampedusa is in the most literal sense an outlier – its population of around 6,000 is far surpassed by the number of people landing in rickety crafts each year. Yet the most remarkable thing is that Matteo Salvini's party has been able to celebrate similar advances in small towns across Italy where immigration is close to nil.

While the Lega (now divested of the qualifier 'Nord') continues to score highest in its historic redoubts, racking up absolute majorities in northeastern Italy, its rise under Salvini has been most notable in its national spread. If in examining the rise of Five Star we highlighted the collapse of the left-wing vote, Salvini's success owes much more to a radicalisation of existing right-wing voters, and collapsing turnout for his rivals. In southern towns, where only five years ago its leaders defined the locals as *terroni*, the Lega has won over the historic Catholic-conservative vote, moreover converting former Berlusconian and postfascist officials into its own cadres. In March 2018, it rose from almost zero to high single figures in the *mezzogiorno*; by May 2019's European election, it came second only to M5S in the south and the islands, where it took over 20 per cent support. This is no uniform picture: the Lega vote remains wealthier and older than the general population; in the south, it is winning more support from other right-wing parties than from the M5S.

Yet this also points to the wider bases of Salvini's success. Left-wing Italians often refer to a Berlusconian *ventennio*, a spell of hegemony implicitly compared to the twenty years of Mussolinian rule. In fact, the media mogul was only prime minister for nine years scattered between 1994 and 2011. But what he did achieve was to dominate the right, gathering provincial business elites and a captive audience of Mediaset-viewing housewives behind his leadership. Amid the splintering of old political identities, Berlusconi's ability to polarise the Second Republic around himself also relied on his ability to play his allies off against one another, maintaining his own role as both king and kingmaker. Yet this approach also drove a wider hegemonic shift. If his TV channels helped promote the imaginary of hard-working entrepreneurs struggling to shake off the encumbrances of the state, this agenda could also be harnessed by other parties.

This, indeed, was the opportunity opened up for the Lega in the post-crisis period. The debt crisis that led to Berlusconi's ouster in September 2011, and even his 2013 ban from public office, at first seemed like bumps along the road in a political career that had faced many sharp reversals and legal troubles. Even on the eve of the 2018 election, polls indicated that Forza Italia would edge out the Lega to remain the biggest party of the centre-right, in an alliance that looked within range of securing a majority of seats. Yet the biggest shock on results night was precisely the fact that Berlusconi's party had lost its hegemony over its brother-enemies. The oldest force represented in parliament, the Lega Nord founded in 1991, had finally secured more votes than Forza Italia. Salvini's victory over the octogenarian fixer would lay the basis for fresh advances in subsequent months. But it was also the culmination of a fight to transform the Lega itself.

As we shall see in this chapter, Matteo Salvini's newly Italian-nationalist Lega is, in many ways, the product of circumstance – and the failure of his opponents – rather than some genial design elaborated in advance. This is particularly notable in the fact that the party's lightning-quick rise (hitting 34 per cent at the May 2019 European election) in fact came mostly after the 2018 general election, at the point that it had finally shown itself able to displace Forza Italia as the leading centre-right force. After Salvini became the Lega's national secretary in late 2013, he succeeded in stabilising the party's structures, but its 6 per cent score in the 2014 European election was an exercise in damage limitation rather than a breakthrough, and right up until the moment of the 2018 general election it was unclear that the Lega was about impose its political hegemony. In the run-up to that contest, press warnings of a looming

Italian break with the euro (or, as this author pointed out, the prospect of a more muddled Eurosceptic government)[1] often pointed to the possibility that Salvini would break from the Berlusconian fold and ally with the M5S. The realisation of such an alliance in June 2018 not only brought the Lega back into government, but helped it to lay the bases of a wider transformation of the right.

In this sense, Salvini's greatest success has been to "nationalise" the Lega, entrenching its control in small towns across its Padanian heartlands while also extending its organisation across regions where it had not even existed in the 1990s and 2000s. In particular, the historic *sorpasso* over Forza Italia in March 2018 – and then the step into a coalition with Luigi di Maio – has allowed the Lega to cannibalise its eternal rival-ally, not only conquering his former electoral redoubts but also drawing former personnel and clientelist networks into Lega structures. Just as in the 1990s Forza Italia and the Alleanza Nazionale integrated formerly Christian-Democratic aligned political bosses, local business figures, and even organised crime into their ranks, under Salvini's leadership the Lega has done the same. As we shall see, these forces' rallying behind the Lega comes with a hefty dose of opportunism; the desire to chase the bandwagon also extended to voters themselves, as within three months of the March 2018 election the Lega had already climbed a further ten points in opinion polls.

The rapid advance of the Lega as well as the circumstantial nature of its rise again point to the intense volatility of post-1992 Italian politics and, indeed, the instability of this new bloc. Throughout his spell as interior minister from June 2018 to August 2019, Salvini became the latest one-man show in Italian politics, using well-orchestrated clashes with

NGOs, Brussels, and migrant-rescue operations in order to push himself to the centre of the political arena. Where, in the 1990s, Berlusconi based his political career on his TV empire and in the 2000s Beppe Grillo built a party around his blog, Salvini's preferred medium is Twitter, as political messaging gets even more individual and, indeed, concise. Salvini has laid the bases for a lasting polarisation in Italian politics, allying the Lega's long-standing tax-cutting, anti-statist, and anti-immigrant agendas with a new, galvanising nationalist thrust. Yet as we shall see in this chapter, the more personality-centric forms the Lega has taken under Salvini's leadership bear contradictions of their own. If the Lega Nord had long built its structures on cadre organisation, similar to that of the mass parties of old, the new Lega appears to have premised its growth on far shakier foundations. At the same time, its historic redoubts in Veneto and Lombardy remain anchored in the separatist traditions of old – a northern-autonomist spirit not easily dissuaded by the party's success at the national level.

Heading South

Salvini's taste for the spotlight was apparent from early in life: already by age twenty-one he had made two separate appearances on TV quiz shows. (Matteo Renzi appeared on *Wheel of Fortune* just once.) A certain legend likes to present Salvini as a disillusioned leftist, tying his party's quest for support among ex-Communist voters to his own youthful visits to the Leoncavallo social centre in Milan. In fact, though as a teenager he occasionally attended concerts in the squat, he was never politically active, and already by age twenty he was a Lega Nord local councillor in Milan. Elected to that role in 1993, he spent the next two decades promoting positions identical to Bossi's own, vaunting his 'Padanian' identity and calling for regions like his own Lombardian homeland to be liberated from the South. Now-embarrassing pictures of Salvini show that he was not always so keen to play the role of the Italian patriot. Not only did he don collared shirts in *leghista* green but so, too, t-shirts declaring 'Padania is not Italy' – written in English, as if in a bid for international recognition. When Italy made the final of the 2006 football World Cup, he proudly declared that he would be supporting France.

Elected to Lega Nord leadership after its rout at the February 2013 general election, where it scored just 4.3 per cent of the vote, Salvini's task was to save the party from outright extinction. Faced with the rise of M5S's online 'revolution', the shrinking band of *leghisti* turning out for the summer fête at Pontida looked even more parochial than usual. But, if popular distaste for Mario Monti's technocratic government had failed to inspire support for the Lega Nord, the convulsions of the more mainstream parties continued to serve up opportunities. This particularly owed to the crisis in Berlusconi's Popolo della Libertà (People of Freedom; PdL) after the election, first entering coalition with the Democrats (PD) then splitting from it in August 2013 when it failed to protect him from his fraud conviction. With this blow, which saw Berlusconi barred from public office, the tycoon also lost control of his party. As we have seen, his long-time protégé Angelino Alfano broke away with all sitting PdL ministers to form Nuovo Centrodestra (New Centre Right), which remained in government together with the Democrats and Monti's Scelta Civica (Civic Choice).

Certainly, there was a broader confusion of political identities. Not only did the upstart M5S claim to stand above left and right, but Alfano's party, the New Centre Right, was now counted in opinion surveys as a 'centre-left' force because of its alliance with the PD. Yet the Lega's own positioning was also in the balance. Since Bossi's hardest oppositional phase in the late 1990s, it had abandoned its secessionist rhetoric, becoming part of a broader centre-right bloc over the 2000s. Taking over the party leadership after Bossi's downfall in 2012, Maroni sought to harden the *leghista* base with a fresh regionalist push, insisting it could play an independent role in the centre-right bloc akin to the pact between Bavaria's Christian Social Union and the German Christian Democrats. If such a proposal implied that the right-wing parties should share out the different regions, Salvini's own project was far more radical – a bid to take the Lega national. Becoming leader at the moment of the Lega's greatest crisis, a man who had spent his life serving Bossi ventured to replace its historic identity with his own.

Noi con Salvini (Us with Salvini) was the first expression of this shift, advancing the Lega into central-southern Italy while also disciplining the party under its new *segretario*. Modest in its initial results, this experience nonetheless showed Salvini's bid both to take his party beyond its historic heartlands and to begin conquering the support of the other right-wing parties. In this he could count on the support of the MP Angelo Attaguile, son of a DC minister and himself that party's youth leader in the 1970s, who defected to the Lega in 2013 after being elected on a Berlusconian list in the Campania region surrounding Naples. While such a profile might point to a classic recycling of personnel among parties, Salvini chose Attaguile to flank him on a visit to Palermo,

Sicily, on 8 February 2015, where, appearing in a 'Sicilia' hoodie,[2] he apologised to Sicilians for past anti-southern rhetoric and insisted that fighting the mafia was his top priority. Insisting that 'he had always attacked *bad politics* in the South', Salvini emphasised law-and-order talking points including a crack-down on black-market farm work.

However, Salvini also mooted a turn into a more conventionally far-right space, pitching his party away from Berlusconi and toward even forces outside the traditional *centrodestra* coalition. This was apparent at the first Noi con Salvini rally in Rome on 28 February 2015, a demonstration against Renzi where the Lega leader spoke alongside Simone Di Stefano, leader of the neofascist Rome social centre CasaPound. This group – of relatively younger and more media-savvy colouration than other neofascist subcultures – even formed a short-lived anti-EU front together with Salvini called Sovranità, though they broke off formal relations later in 2015. Less of a radical step was the presence at the rally of Giorgia Meloni, leader of Fratelli d'Italia, a historical descendant of the Movimento Sociale Italiano – Alleanza Nazionale. In the 2016 regional election in Lazio (the region surrounding Rome), Noi con Salvini made its first major electoral push as part of Meloni's campaign.[3] However, it made an only very tentative breakthrough: in the capital the party's candidates, headed by former Lega parliamentary speaker Irene Pivetti, scored 2.7 per cent out of the 20.6 per cent that went to Meloni's alliance, and, in other small towns, it similarly scored in very low single figures.

The party's path into southern and central Italy met with resistance, from both within and outside Lega ranks. Salvini's first appearance in Palermo was met with a demonstration (as well as a hail of eggs and rotten vegetables), and even right-wingers who remembered Salvini's use of the racist term *terroni* for southerners were not necessarily well disposed to his new, more 'inclusive' nationalism. Noi con Salvini also lacked party structures in southern regions, instead basing itself on the public profile of former DC and Forza Italia bosses integrated into its ranks like Attaguile and the less-than-squeaky-clean Sicilian regional deputy Tony Rizzotto. Nonetheless, Salvini also attempted to emphasise how he differed from the parties of the Second Republic. He emphasised the historic importance of his 'anti-corruption' agenda, including through his repeated insistence that the Lega did not want any further alliance with Berlusconi.[4] Asked by a reporter how he could counterpose the Lega Nord to Forza Italia when Bossi had himself fallen to an embezzlement conviction, Salvini blandly insisted that he could take no responsibility for the choices made in different times.

The Lega's move beyond its heartlands was not just a matter of heading into the South. The decision to stand across Italy was decisive for changing the overall profile of the party, including by shifting from a regionalist to a more pointedly nationalist, Eurosceptic, and anti-immigrant agenda. Yet the Lega also needed to hegemonise the right in parts of central-northern Italy that had long been redoubts of the left. In the electoral maps of the First Republic, the so-called regioni rosse of Emilia-Romagna, Tuscany, Marche, and Umbria had often been the only ones coloured in the red of the Partito Comunista Italiano, historic heartlands of the labour movement even unto the nineteenth century. Yet there had always been middle-class, Catholic, and conservative voters in these regions, and with the weakening of Berlusconi, the Lega hoped to rally them under its own leadership. After overtaking Forza Italia in the 2014 regional vote in Emilia-Romagna, in 2015 the Lega headed joint lists together with the postfascist Fratelli d'Italia (Brothers of Italy; FdI) in Tuscany (scoring 16 per cent, up from 6.5 per cent in 2010) and Marche (13 per cent, up from 6 per cent in 2010), while also becoming the biggest force in the *centrodestra* bloc in Umbria.

The Lega's advance in these regional elections mostly owed to a changing power balance – a radicalisation process – within the centre-right, rather than the conquest of former left-wing voters themselves. At best, it could count on high rates of abstention by voters once loyal to the Communist Party and its successors. At the same time, while the symbolism of the Lega extending its reach into former PCI heartlands was impressive (and widely noted),[5] its rise in these contests was actually far smaller than the losses for Berlusconi. This dynamic was visible even in the Lega's own northern redoubts. In Veneto in 2015, the *leghista* president Luca Zaia was re-elected on 50.1 per cent support: the Lega vote held firm at almost 800,000, but the almost 500,000 votes lost by Berlusconi meant that Zaia dropped 10.1 per cent overall. In historically less favourable Liguria, the Lega nearly doubled its score from 10.2 to 20.3 per cent, decisively aiding the election of a Forza Italia president, Giovanni Toti; yet the centre-right as a whole fell from 47.8 to 34.4 per cent, with both main blocs leaking support to the M5S and abstention. Standing for the first time, the M5S was by far the most dynamic force in these regional contests, not winning any presidencies but doing much to tear voters away from the main centre-left and centre-right blocs.

The Lega had outcompeted Forza Italia across northern Italy and the former *regioni rosse*, but not proven able to form an independent bloc in the manner of M5S. Instead, amidst talk of an early general election, Salvini turned back toward an alliance of the right. Such a vote could not take place immediately: back in 2014 the Constitutional Court had struck down the electoral system used since 2006, deeming unconstitutional its pretension to guarantee a majority to the largest coalition. The political momentum behind the call for a new voting system also owed to the result of the 2013 general election, where the malfunctioning of this system in the Senate race had led to no overall control – and hence a grand coalition. Discussions of such a reform were thus again a key focus of this legislature. First, this served as Renzi's means of bringing Berlusconi back into the political fray in 2014 (the so-called 'Nazareno Pact'), as he sought an ally to push through a more binary system. However, by 2017, the Lega had decisively swung behind this project, and by October a new, more majoritarian system had been formulated. This system promised to distribute 61 per cent of seats in the Chamber of Deputies on the basis of first-past-the-post, in a change widely expected to help consolidate the centre-left and centre-right blocs. Only the M5S opposed this, fearing it would lose out most in three-way contests.

But if the right saw the need for unity, it was unclear who would lead it. The historic candidate Berlusconi announced his return to the fray in March 2017, seeking to be the centre-right candidate for premier despite his ban from public office. This earned short shrift from the Lega, no longer willing to play second fiddle. Yet, while Salvini publicly toyed with the idea of running separately, both the majoritarian logic of the electoral system and the results of the December 2017 Sicilian election – where a fragmentary right-wing alliance surprisingly defeated M5S – showed that this was not a serious prospect. What postfascist Fratelli d'Italia leader Meloni called the 'arancino pact' for the Sicilian contest was in fact a dry run for a national-level alliance for the general election of 4 March 2018. Berlusconi was still a powerful force, thanks to his media empire – he now played the role of penitent sinner, loving grandfather and animal lover, seeking redemption after his ills with the courts. Yet he had lost his hegemonic role in the right-wing alliance – Salvini slapped down his plans to name a loyal 'proxy' who would serve as premier in his place. If Forza Italia posters incongruously called for 'Berlusconi presidente', the Lega instead put forward the name of its own leader.

Blood on Their Hands

In the build-up to the general election, international media attention was less focused on the rise of the right as a possible crisis event – the possibility that anti-euro parties were on the brink of power. While Berlusconi had fallen out of favour with European centre-right figures like Angela Merkel at the height of the sovereign debt crisis in 2011, he now presented himself in the guise of an 'anti-populist' defender of Europeanism, both opening up to a deal with the PD and reining in the Lega's radical impulses. The logic of alliance with Salvini held firm – the first-past-the-post element of the new electoral system rewarded coalitions, and thus encouraged the formation of a broad right. Yet with seats distributed among the individual parties, there was no necessary bind between pre-election coalitions and the alliances that might take form in parliament afterward. The campaign was thus marked by intense press speculation on how far these coalitions would last after polling day itself. Polls showed that both Democratic and Forza Italia voters favoured a coalition of the anti-populist centre – a term now widely assumed to include Berlusconi as well as the main centre-left party. For his part, Luigi di Maio threatened to get in the way of such plans by mooting an alliance plan of his own: while he insisted he did not seek coalitions, he also made vaguer references to the possibility of deals with the Lega, the centre-left Liberi o Uguali (Free and Equal),[6] or even the PD 'without Renzi' – so long as they agreed to implement M5S's own agenda.[7]

Thus, already before the election, there emerged the prospect of a future realignment, entrenching a new divide between liberalism (as represented by the PD and Forza Italia) and Euroscepticism (as represented by M5S and the Lega). The financial press warned that the uncertainties of Italian politics could create the next crisis event in the euro – or even a mandate for an outright Italexit. Yet upon closer inspection, the outsiders besieging the political centre were not so committed to leaving the euro after all. In previous years, the M5S had gone so far as to call for a referendum on the single currency (though not actually advocate a euro exit); by the end of 2017, it abruptly dropped this demand, even deleting the webpage that had once hosted a petition to this effect. Under Bossi's leadership, the Lega Nord had at first enthusiastically championed the notion of a European Padania, but once Italy was on course for eurozone membership it dropped this line and had adopted Eurosceptic positions. This reached its peak in November 2013 as new leader Matteo Salvini held a 'No Euro Day' rally together with anti-euro economists Claudio Borghi and Alberto Bagnai.

However, it too faced internal dramas over this policy, not least given the damage that exit would do to savers and German-facing businesses. Despite his overt enthusiasm for the blow that Brexit struck to European liberalism, Salvini used the alliance with Berlusconi as a pretext to back away from any talk of Italexit.

The specifically European dimension of the election instead related to immigration, identified by the Lega as a product of Italian elites' collusion with Brussels. Refugee numbers had rising salience from 2013 onward, especially due to the human flight driven by the Syrian and Libyan civil wars; while in that year the Letta government had launched a search-and-rescue operation in the Mediterranean, called Mare Nostrum, it was abandoned within a year, as Renzi claimed that Europe as a whole had to take responsibility. This was partially realised by the EU's Frontex, replacing Mare Nostrum with a mission more directed at keeping refugees away from Italy – and less to saving lives at sea. In tandem with this, European authorities sought to outsource the repression of migration, through the EU's 2016 deal with Turkey and, in 2017, PD interior minister Marco Minniti's similar deal with Libya. This extended apparatus of repression, and indeed the rhetoric by M5S leader Luigi Di Maio (condemning the perilous refugee voyages across the Mediterranean as NGO-operated 'migrant taxis') fed the intensifying anti-immigration mood. But it was Salvini who focused most exclusively and consistently on this theme, serving as the glue of his party's newfound Italian nationalism. It served as the framing device for all the other themes he advanced, from the unaccountability of EU institutions to rising criminality, the fecklessness of Italian elites, and the corruption of NGOs ('fake cooperatives') supporting migrants.

Salvini's success on this terrain accelerated even after the PD-led government had begun to radically reduce migrant numbers; it had more to do with a successful marketing operation – and the weak opposition to his narrative – than to the material effects of migration. This particularly owed to his skill in promoting under-exposed cases of criminal activity by migrants, or what were in fact small scandals in isolated towns, as indicative of the general realities that Italians had to face and the political authorities' failure in doing anything about them. This was allied to a structural critique of unfairness in the sharing-out of migrants among European countries, and in particular the Dublin Agreement, which obliges the states where asylum applicants are first registered (largely meaning states on the shores and outer borders of the EU) to handle their claims and thus to provide for them so long as their claims are being reviewed. Indeed, even as the number of arrivals fell steeply (dropping from 181,436 in 2016 to 119,247 in 2017, according to UNHCR data, and then from 24,278 to 6,161 in the first quarter of 2018), Salvini insisted that Italy was being overrun. These numbers were around half to two-thirds as high as the number of Italians emigrating.

There was, however, little sign of push-back from elsewhere on the political spectrum. The pervasive racism of Italian society – combatted by NGOs, a small activist left and some Catholic forces – was typified in the final business of the 2013–18 legislature. Here, the PD-led government made a strikingly half-hearted effort to institute so-called *ius soli*, that is, granting citizenship to the children of non-citizens born on Italian soil (of whom there are currently around 800,000). The main explicit opposition came from the right-wing parties, though its passage through parliament failed only thanks to abstention, thanks to twenty-nine PD senators and thirty-five from M5S (its entire Senate group), none of whom backed the bill. The Lega's response to this debate was, indeed, a particularly harsh instance of its chauvinism. Seeking to deny not only citizenship to the children of immigrants born in Italy, but basic public services. Such was the case of the Lega mayor of Lodi, in its historic heartlands in Lombardy. In November 2017 she issued a decree to stop non–European Union citizens using school buses or taking school meals: most of those affected were born in Italy, but nonetheless had to suffer because their parents were African.

Salvini's anti-immigrant line would also play a dominant role in the election campaign itself. This was most dramatically illustrated by the political response to a terrorist attack which took place in Macerata, in the Marche region, on 3 February 2018. In this drive-by shooting – just five weeks before the election – the white supremacist Luca Traini opened fire at a group of African migrants before then turning his weapon on the local PD office. Six people were injured. Upon his arrest, Traini had an Italian flag around his shoulders and gave a fascist salute: he told police he was taking 'revenge' after the murder of a local eighteen-year-old by a failed Nigerian asylum seeker. It soon turned out that he had previously stood as a Lega Nord candidate in local elections. While anti-racist groups were quick to highlight the climate of rising violence (and indeed Traini's own neo-Nazi and *leghista* ties), the main political reaction focused rather more on the 'insecurity' that had so enraged Traini. Renzi insisted that 'Italy and Italians ought to be defended by the police, not gunmen,'[8] whereas Interior Minister Minniti claimed he had reduced migration in order 'to avoid this kind of attack'.[9] Salvini put the same message in stronger terms, adding 'clearly, uncontrolled immigration, an invasion like the one organised, willed and financed in recent years, will lead to social strife.'[10]

The harsh debate on mass immigration – presented by all major parties as a central cause of crime – allowed the Lega to polarise the right-wing electorate around its identitarian agenda, while also promoting it to the cutting edge of the fight against 'the left'. The fact that the shooting had been perpetrated by a Lega member did nothing to undermine the party's polling numbers, which remained around four points behind Forza Italia. If anything, the attack served its intended purpose of radicalisation, prompting Berlusconi himself to take a sharper line, precisely in order to head off the competition from the Lega. In a characteristically bombastic announcement, the oft-convicted magnate called for the imminent removal of 600,000 undocumented immigrants from Italy, claiming that the 'left-wing governments of recent years' had allowed 'the creation of a social bomb', given the 'propensity of migrants to commit crimes'.[11] Yet, while Forza Italia's owner-operator also stressed more 'centrist'-sounding measures, including a 'Marshall Plan for Africa' to slow migration, the Lega adopted harsher tones toward other political forces, claiming that the PD had 'blood on its hands' for allowing mass immigration into Italy.

Anatomy of the Vote

The first results on the night of 4 March 2018 were a shock. Both insurgent parties did better than polls had forecast, and there was an even-bigger-than-expected collapse of the centre. The big winner was M5S, whose 32 per cent score outstripped all polling predictions. While the PD slumped to 18 per cent, a historic low, and further-left forces scored miserably, the biggest surprise was on the right. The *centrodestra*'s overall 37 per cent score was in line with most polling, but the big news of the 'Maratona Mentana' results programme on TG La7 was the shift within the right-wing bloc. Whereas polls had consistently shown Matteo Salvini's party just behind Forza Italia, the Lega ultimately edged out Berlusconi's party, by 17.4 to 14 per cent of the vote. This was the first time that the Lega had ever been the biggest right-wing party in a national election. At first it was impossible to tell how a government could be formed, with the Democrats and Forza Italia well short of the seats to form a grand coalition and an overall picture of fragmentation. But with the Lega and M5S totalling over half the seats, it would be impossible to form a coalition that excluded both.

As in the 2013 contest, and indeed the political revolution of 1994, in the 2018 general election Italians dealt an enormous blow to the previously dominant parties. But this did not make clear what kind of change they wanted. In the first election of the Second Republic it had been the forces of the right that exploited the anti-corruption mood, stopping the ex-Communist PDS in its tracks, whereas in the 2013 contest the M5S was the only truly dynamic force. This time, two different radicalisms had each benefited at the expense of those parties that conceived themselves as more moderate and centrist. Doubtless, both had mobilised discontent with the handling of the economic crisis as well as immigration. Yet the parties that won on 4 March were not united by any common (or even clear) positions on Europe, and, in economic terms, they stood in outright contradiction. While both promised to reduce the retirement age, M5S's guarantee of benefit payments for jobseekers seemed hard to square with the Lega's call for a 15 per cent flat tax, threatening to wipe as much as €100 billion out of state coffers.

The social base of the two insurgent parties also presented many – and connected – differences, mapping onto the divide between the relatively more welfarist M5S and the sharply tax-cutting Lega. Indeed, according to pollster Ipsos's post-election data, the M5S vote was much stronger among public sector employees (41.6 per cent) than among their private sector counterparts (34 per cent), while the Lega instead had an even more marked bias in the opposite direction. It took an estimated 18.7 per cent among private sector workers, as against 12.8 per cent in the public sector. Its vote among *operai e affini* (a loose collection of blue-collar and manual jobs; 23.8 per cent) was actually slightly higher than its vote among small businessmen, traders, and artisans (23.6 per cent); white-collar and state employees were, in contrast, its second-weakest category apart from entrepreneurs and top managers (12.9 per cent). In age terms, M5S's vote in fact became more homogeneous relative to the previous contest in 2013, as it tripled its support among pensioners (to 26.4 per cent, only one point behind the PD, top in this category).[12] Its average voter was, nonetheless, around a decade younger than her *leghista* counterpart.

Also useful in the Ipsos study was its indication of electoral shifts – who was losing votes to whom, compared to the last contest in 2013, and which parties had instead managed to maintain their previous base. Remarkable here was the collapse in the PD vote after its years in government, as just 43 per cent of its 2013 electorate again turned out for the party in 2018. This did not, however, mean that the centre-left vote directly defected to the populist right. The biggest other choices were either to abstain (as did 22 per cent of 2013 PD voters) or vote M5S (14 per cent); in fact, more of the remainder headed to other, more-left-wing parties than to the Lega (which garnered a mere 2 per cent of these recent PD supporters). Far more stable was M5S, which maintained 76 per cent of its 2013 electorate; it lost 9 per cent to abstention, while picking up the highest support among 2013 non-voters. But especially notable here was the source of Lega votes, which were overwhelmingly drawn from other right-wing parties and not from either the left or M5S . Of those who had voted for the right-wing coalition five years ago, some 41 per cent opted for the Lega, as against 33 per cent for Forza Italia and 8 per cent for the M5S. Meanwhile, just 6 per cent of 2013 M5S voters turned to the Lega. On 4 March 2018, the rise of Salvini's party owed far more to switchers within the right-wing bloc – to the collapse of Berlusconi – than to any other dynamic.

Such data also rather question the idea that the Lega has become the new 'workers' party' or indeed taken over former 'red bastions'. Without doubt, such analyses bear some elements of insight insofar as they identify the class shift within the centre-left, falling far behind the Lega and especially M5S among such groups as blue-collar workers and the unemployed. Yet the territorial and sectoral distribution of this vote suggests that the Lega is doing little to pick up disgruntled former left-wingers, instead basing its support on a radicalisation of a pre-existing right-wing base. Unlike the traditional base of Italian labour, which is far more likely to vote M5S or abstain, the blue-collar Lega vote instead seems to conform more to the pattern suggested by Amable and Palombarini, where workers in small and medium-sized businesses suffered the effects of the euro in tandem with their under-pressure bosses. This reading is also borne out by pollster SWG's data for 1987 voters (Table 2.3) which show the Lega in second place among former DC voters in 2018 (20 per cent) but only fourth among those who used to back the PCI (9 per cent). In this general election as in local and regional contests that followed, the Lega repainted many old red fortresses in its own dark green. But its greatest ally here was not so much its own efforts to pick up former left-wing voters, but the fact that these latter were no longer voting all.

Imposing Hegemony

Thus far, we have focused on the processes that destabilised the parties of the Second Republic, allowing the Five Star Movement and the Lega to make their respective break-throughs in the 2013 and 2018 general elections. Whereas M5S was best able to rally voters discontented with the centre-left and, more broadly, mobilise a transversal rejection of established political codes, the Lega's success lay above all in the radicalisation of the right. Yet since this election result, in which two outsider forces together took 50 per cent of the vote, they have developed in wholly different directions. Earlier we noted political scientist Ilvo Diamanti's comments to the effect that, even when faced with a crisis in the structures of political representation, it is also important to explain what characteristics of any particular insurgent makes it better able than others to impose itself as an alternative. In our contention, this applies not only to the outsider's initial electoral rise, but also its ability to form an enduring hegemony, not only meeting the test of institutional power but also recomposing the wider political field. The experience of the two populist parties since March 2018, and especially since they formed a government at the beginning of that June, is a striking illustration of this problem. Whereas the eclectic Five Star Movement immediately began to fragment along its own internal fault lines, Salvini's Lega has used its more coherent organisation to consolidate its power.

These different trajectories were, in fact, apparent even during the coalition negotiations themselves. The M5S had never before entered into local or regional-level alliances – its leader Luigi di Maio insisted before the election that he would only be willing to accept support from forces who signed up to M5S's own programme. But its party's surprisingly strong result compelled it to take the leading role in forming a new government. Given the new parliamentary arithmetic, it was impossible for any majority to be formed that excluded *both* the M5S and the Lega. This soon resolved itself into two alternative sets of coalition negotiations led by Di Maio, what he termed the 'two stoves' he was each heating up. On the one hand was the prospect of a deal between the M5S and the centre-right – a prospect confirmed when parliament reconvened at the start of April, and these forces voted to distribute the institutionally important speakers' roles among themselves. Yet keen not to be seen to be tacking to the right, Di Maio also publicly maintained negotiations with the PD.

Some prominent M5S supporters in the media did support this latter course of action – notably the investigative newspaper *Il Fatto Quotidiano*, many of whose personnel come from left-wing backgrounds. Yet M5S's origins as a revolt against the *casta* made such an arrangement unlikely – indeed, the PD was reluctant to embrace such a hostile force as the M5S, which it had itself long characterised as anti-democratic and Europhobic. After a bruising electoral loss, the PD could little risk playing second fiddle to the M5S – which would have further diluted its own coherence. Former prime minister Matteo Renzi, a continual eminence grise, colourfully suggested that the PD would benefit more from seeing the M5S and Lega tested in government – he wanted to 'sit back with the popcorn and watch' the twin populists in power.[13] As for Salvini, his attitude was shaped by his determination to consolidate his position as new leader of the right-wing bloc, after having surprisingly outscored Berlusconi's Forza Italia in the election. For the Lega leader, it would be unthinkable to serve only as a junior partner to the M5S. If he did bring his party into government, it would have to be on equal terms – and take place with the tacit consent of his right-wing allies.

Decisive, in this regard, was the mechanism of a 'contract', discussed by the M5S and the Lega. From Di Maio's point of view, this served as a kind of defence from the accusation that his party had pitched toward the right. Rather than seek a coalition with the Lega, he insisted that all that was on the agenda was a short-term transaction, in which they would divide up control of ministries and the national government agenda among themselves, but without agreeing to any wider political alliance – for instance, such as might have implied collaboration in regional or local elections and councils. Indeed, the Lega would remain part of the right-wing bloc at these levels, even though neither Forza Italia or the postfascists would make up part of the governmental majority nationally. At the same time, the contract would include campaign promises from both the M5S and Lega, now made policy. With the small problem that the policies written into the contract were incompatible, the entire document uncosted. Thus the Lega's call for a 15 per cent flat tax rate was accompanied by the M5S's plans for a 'citizens' income' for the unemployed.

Yet other elements of the negotiations – and the deal – showed how much M5S was outflanked by Salvini. Whereas it secured no specific commitments for regeneration in its own southern heartlands, the Lega's commitment to greater autonomy for northern regions was mentioned. A notional commitment to renegotiating Italy's debt with the European Union remained sufficiently vague as to placate both sides. But the appointment of ministers played heavily in the Lega's favour. In a bid to make sure neither party leader dominated the coalition, the chosen prime minister was the independent Giuseppe Conte. A non-party law professor without a base in parliament, he was in fact such an unknown that he had no Wikipedia page prior to discussion of his likely premiership (a clear case of the M5S's desire to frustrate journalists). The slated foreign minister was Enzo Moavero Milanesi, an independent and career technocrat who had been European affairs minister under the Monti and Letta administrations of the early 2010s. Other choices were more political – Di Maio would be labour minister, in a bid to cement M5S's position as the party of workers. Yet two other roles did far more to set the government's agenda. First was the Interior Ministry – handed to Salvini personally. After an election campaign that the Lega had fought on a harsh law-and-order programme directed mainly against immigrants, this brief offered Salvini a perfect tribune to galvanise his own base – and use it to build his popularity among supporters of the other right-wing parties with no similar platform.

Paradoxically, perhaps even more decisive was the selection of economy minister. In late May, some eleven weeks after the general election itself, the new administration was

ready to go – with Paolo Savona mooted to take charge of
the nation's finances. As in the case of the prime minister's
office and the Foreign Ministry, this role was to be handed to
a non-party man. Savona may not have seemed an especially
conspicuous choice: a professional economist rather than an
elected politician, he had been industry minister in the technocratic cabinet of 1993–4 and then led relations between
Berlusconi's government and EU institutions in the mid-
2000s. Yet his selection soon threatened to collapse the
M5S-Lega deal, as President of the Republic Sergio Mattarella
refused to sign off on his nomination. Insisting on the need
to uphold Italy's commitment to Europe, Mattarella's outriders insisted that Savona's Euroscepticism – expressed in an
old academic paper where he speculated on how Italy could
secretly prepare an overnight break with the eurozone –
risked taking the government far further than voters had
ever given it a mandate for. This unprecedented decision was
nonetheless shocking – the centre-left *L'Espresso* magazine
spoke of the 'darkest moment in the history of the republic'.[14] If its editor here referred to the impasse rather than
Mattarella's move as such, others across the political spectrum cast it as undemocratic – placing European criteria as a
barrier to the parliamentary majority.

This crisis brilliantly demonstrated Salvini's strengths.
After recent days of news coverage in which Paris's *Le Monde*
had caricatured Italy as a baby at the European table,
Frankfurt's *FAZ* termed it 'Europe's problem child' and
Berlin's *Der Spiegel* denounced a land of 'aggressive beggars',[15]
the condemnation of the looming 'populist experiment' was
already sending exactly the message that the Lega leader
wanted. But the rejection of the Eurosceptic finance minister posed the problem even more concretely – even without

ever committing himself to any specific policy regarding Italy's relations with Europe, Salvini could damn European and local elites' determination to block the popular will. As President Mattarella instead began the process of forming an alternative government – handing an exploratory mandate to centrist-neoliberal economist Carlo Cottarelli, the Lega soared in the polls. Surveys the following day showed that Salvini's party had jumped three points in a week – now standing at 27.5 per cent, just two points behind M5S. As the country careered toward a fresh general election, it looked as if the same contest was about to be played out again, yet with Salvini poised to make yet further gains.

It remains to be known how far the selection of Savona was a deliberate provocation. After a few days of scandal-mongering, Salvini dropped the mooted finance minister in favour of the rather less Eurosceptic economist Giovanni Tria. By June 1, the government was ready to form, with no other changes to its composition or government 'contract'. Yet already in this crisis Salvini had illustrated the basic dynamics that would shape the two parties' spell in office, with M5S struggling to communicate the same identitarian message as the Lega leader himself. Di Maio's response to Mattarella's decision was, certainly, a vehement denuncia-tion, even calling for impeachment (which nothing in the Constitution provided for). He moreover communicated a sense of shock at the purported thwarting of democratic choice, supposedly suppressed by Brussels. Yet whereas he protested in vain, he also knew that early elections were not an option – for their only effect would be to strengthen Salvini, now bidding for hegemony of the whole centre-right bloc. Also remarkable, here, was how little the Lega leader had ever risked. He had asserted himself as a national leader, aggressively defending Italy's right to defy the European Union. But he had done so without actually insisting on the need to keep Savona – or ever specifying that the Lega did indeed seek a break with the eurozone.

On 1 June 2018, the independent prime minister Giuseppe Conte's government was finally sworn in. Even when his name first began circulating on 21 May, it was widely assumed that he would not really be in charge of his cabinet. By the end of the month, the first signs were already emerging that the M5S would not be, either. In government, Salvini dominated the Lega's communications, constantly imposing his own dividing lines on the whole political terrain. Where this strongman nationalist used his visibility to assert his leadership, the eclectic M5S instead found that its contradictions had become plain to see.

Making the Lega Italia

The Lega leader's communicative style was doubtless a key element in helping him exploit the post-election negotiations, and the crisis around Savona, to his own benefit. This was, indeed, a much-vaunted element of Salvini's spell in government, in which he used his platform in the Interior Ministry to rile up his own base and to troll his opponents. This was particularly effective when it came to his dramatisation of migrant arrivals via social media, issuing tweets in order to order the closing of the ports. Such a power does not, in fact, lie in the hands of the interior minister; Salvini nonetheless managed to confect an image of robust authority by constantly having himself photographed in police uniform. As journalist Matteo Pucciarelli writes in an insightful piece on 'Salvini ascendant',[16] this communications strategy was also able to exploit M5S's own deeper political weakness. Ater years in which it had itself made 'propaganda against a maritime "invasion"', M5S was 'constrain[ed] to follow the League onto the terrain most favourable to it, with occasional ineffective remonstrations against particularly crude gestures of xenophobia'.[17] This was especially concretised in the behaviour of the figure who did have the power to close the ports – M5S's Danilo Toninelli, infrastructure minister. Bound by loyalty to his coalition partner and M5S's own more evasive politics, he turned Salvini's tweets into government decrees without so much as a discussion, while also shying from the 'credit' for blocking migrants, which instead went to the Lega leader.

The much-heralded closing of the ports was a particularly remarkable piece of theatre. After all, it was never a full-fledged policy, blocking each and every arrival, but rather a series of media stunts by which Salvini picked fights with a small minority of the crews bringing refugees to Italy. Particularly significant was the case of the *Diciotti* coast-guard vessel. In August 2018, just weeks into the new government's spell in office, this boat approached Sicily, with 177 migrants on board; Salvini announced that it would be refused permission to dock. Four months later, prosecutors in Agrigento launched charges against the interior minister for illegal kidnapping, setting up the Lega leader for a further stunt: as Pucciarelli explains, 'When Salvini was informed by the attorney's office in Palermo that he was under indictment for his abandonment of migrants rescued by the Italian coast-guard vessel Diciotti, he recorded the moment by opening the official notification on Facebook Live, where it was viewed 1.1 million times, prompting 111,000 responses in the form of emoticons expressing pleasure, anger, surprise, sadness, 82,000 comments and 25,000 shares. On Twitter his supporters' hashtag #complicediSalvini elicited 192 tweets and 833 re-tweets per hour'.[18] He could, however, count on parliament's ability to screen him from trial; fearing that the government might collapse, should he be hauled before the courts, Five Star voted in the Senate to save him from prosecution. So much for cleaning up politics.

Not only was the M5S craven in the face of Salvini's agenda – swallowing his harsh anti-immigrant line, but also his budget-slashing flat-tax policy – but it also began seeping votes to the strengthening Lega. As we have noted, only a tiny proportion of left-wing voters had switched to Salvini's party in the 2018 general election: only 2 per cent of 2013 PD voters did so, and the M5S was by far the stronger force among the social categories traditionally associated with the Socialist and Communist left. Yet after the government actually took form – and the M5S began to become a loyal accomplice to the Lega – it also became apparent that the 'neither left nor right' party could itself serve as a kind of gateway drug. M5S had not just benefited from the weakening of the PD, but mobilised the former base of the centre-left behind a different politics, determined neither by 'progressive' cultural values or working-class material interest. Yet with the government's immediate agenda dominated by migration, voters who had now broken from the left in favour of the M5S started to turn to the real thing. In the local elections held on 10 and 24 June 2018 the M5S had already begun to stand down some of its own candidates, in favour of the Lega. Some leaders even decided to wash their hands of the government – from parliamentary speaker Roberto Fico, who expressed dissent toward Salvini, to Alessandro di Battista, who headed on a world tour.

In the aftermath of the general election in March, the Lega's advance over Forza Italia had immediately brought a surge in the polls, as the voters of the *centrodestra* began to coalesce around the single biggest centre-right party. Yet there were also tricky tests ahead for the Lega, not least surrounding the European question. This theme particularly encapsulated the different economic priorities of the two parties, given that M5S's main priority was a promise of citizens' income – in reality, something more like Jobseekers' Allowance than an unconditional universal basic income – whereas the Lega promised tax cuts. Salvini's advantage, here, was that he was never forced to choose between the two: rather, his party remained largely silent about welfare spending, while explicitly insisting that Italy should not be dictated to by the EU. The question of sovereignty could thus be pushed onto a more cultural or identitarian terrain, with the actual economic-policy questions affected by the eurozone architecture remaining in the background. This issue was concretised in December 2018, as the government submitted budget plans to Brussels which counted on a 2.4 per cent budget deficit – within the 3 per cent maximum, but still not enough to convince European authorities (or indeed, Finance Minister Tria) of Italy's commitment to reduce its debt. Farcically, a compromise was reached allowing for a 2.04 per cent deficit – perhaps sounding similar enough to those who weren't paying attention. Salvini put up no real resistance, but he did assert his own quasi-presidential role, offering to fly to Brussels to resolve the budget talks – despite the fact that he was interior minister. Again, Salvini was pulling an old trick of the Lega's – acting as if the opposition, even while in government. Yet where Bossi had counterposed the regional to the national, Salvini also staged battles with the EU.

Whereas the Lega's base was galvanised by such antics – more bark than bite – the M5S instead found itself thrown from one crisis to another. Such a baleful experience in government was not, in fact, entirely new to the movement. In local government, it had suffered similarly, proving to be more changed by the constraints of institutional power than itself able to override them. Already in Rome, where Virginia Raggi had been elected mayor in June 2016, the M5S had lurched between disasters, governed by either incompetence or inscrutability; Rome's first citizen suffered not only a continual crisis over waste disposal but also a spate of fires on public transport and even a kickbacks scandal surrounding one of her closest aides. Not only had this damaged the M5S's image of propriety – forcing the party to abandon its own anti-corruption charter regarding its officials' conduct – but it had already produced electoral setbacks, shedding votes in the capital even amid its broader successes at the March 2018 general election. Similarly patchy was her M5S counterpart Chiara Appendino's record as mayor of Turin, facing an embezzlement inquiry of her own, as well as having to back down over the movement's historic opposition to the TAV rail line between Genoa and Lyon. In both cases, a lack of clear political direction meant that the supposed 'anti-corruption' movement was judged on its own preferred criteria of honesty and probity – and the results were not impressive.

The effect of these combined phenomena was that the Lega had already in the early months of the coalition begun to extend its support into new territories, capturing support not only from the other right-wing parties but also from

M5S itself. These successes were particularly remarkable insofar as they often represented non-'Padanian' regions where the old Lega Nord had not previously put up candidates in comparable elections, before its Italian nationalist turn. Already on 22 April 2018, in the weeks following the general election, the Lega had risen from 0 to 8 per cent in the central Italian region of Molise; yet more impressive were its scores in French-speaking Val d'Aoste on 20 May – where it took 17 per cent, standing for the first time – and then in largely German-speaking Trentino–Alto Adige, where the Lega rose from 6 to 11 per cent in the contest held on 21 October. At the same time, nationwide polls had already by the end of July 2018 begun to show the Lega as the largest single party, even surpassing a third of the vote nationally – a force able to begin extending its spread even into the unlikeliest of regions. The Italian nationalist party was now becoming more genuinely national in its organisation, not least as cadres from other right-wing parties began to flock to its banner.

This also posed problems of organisation. The general tendency under Salvini's leadership has been to intensify the centrality of the leader's personal media platform, unknown even in the Bossi era. For now, at least, newfound Lega members could count on Salvini as a winner. Yet alongside the opportunism of many belated leghisti, there was also an unmistakeable element of carpet-bagging, as figures from the North moved to become local Lega bosses in these same territories. In the March 2018 general election Salvini had himself been elected as one of the MPs for Calabria, the southernmost region of mainland Italy. But parallel to this was what Susanna Turco called the rise of the Lega Sudista: the recycling of personnel from other parties, now confected into a southern-based force realising the original plans of Noi con Salvini.[19] Hence the former Lega secretary in Varese (a province bordering Switzerland) headed down to Sicily to take over a local party run by former officials of the old Christian Democracy and Forza Italia; in the words of journalist Antonio Fraschilla, they had followed the Sicilian bourgeoisie's old tradition of 'jumping on the bandwagon.' Former fascists, local political bosses from across the political spectrum, and even circles bound to organised crime, all joined the race to become local Lega officials – in a nationalist force that no longer excluded them from the Padanian community.

Earlier we pointed to the Lega's territorial organisation as a strength. In this sense, it is is yet to complete its transformation into a truly Italian force, or indeed one that can survive setbacks in Salvini's own leadership. His flaunting of both nationalist kitsch and the rosary beads may aid his drive into the South, yet in the party's most-rooted heartlands, it is instead the regionalist cause which still counts for most. This also created tensions with M5S, not least in the government plan, announced at the start of 2019, for 'differentiated autonomy': a proposal that would hand greater powers to some of the richest regions of Italy (the Lega heartlands of Veneto and Lombardy, as well as Emilia-Romagna), while also ensuring that those which paid more in taxes would also be able to spend more. Salvini also sought to extend federalism beyond the North, notably with an alliance with the eclectic Sardinian Action Party, victorious in the February 2019 regional elections. Yet the project is not so easily rolled out everywhere. For as poorer regions and those with more rural populations know, they will be relatively disadvantaged if the Lega allows its own home regions to keep more of their tax take. Thus even as Salvini's nationalist leadership took the party to previously unknown heights, it also created a potential fault-line in Lega ranks, with the demands of regional bosses like Veneto's Luca Zaia or Lombardy's Attilio Fontana standing at odds with any more inclusive national project.

Salvini's nationalist project has, without a doubt, marked an extraordinary development in the Lega. The power of the deep-rooted cadre party of the North has now been projected across the peninsula – in part by the extension of its historic territorial model, but far more so by Salvini's presence as a media figure. As we have described in this book, the suddenness of this breakthrough is not itself surprising, amid the wider climate of volatility – the advances for the Five Star Movement in the great turnover election of 2013, or indeed Berlusconi at the dawn of the Second Republic, were just as impressive. But herein lies a danger for the Lega. In Susanna Turco's words, the new arrivals in Lega ranks 'seem rather like a wave like that of the Forza Italia in 1994, the stunning success that then develops into an organised force'.[20] A harsh nationalism and anti-immigration sentiment do seem, for now, to provide a glue for the Lega's different souls. Yet the Lega has always also fought for a certain set of material demands, and its balancing act between contradictory and often evasive positions on the eurozone, on public spending and on welfare is far from guaranteed to last. In his first year and a half in government, Salvini appeared as if all-powerful, even while maintaining an oppositional stance. What remains to be seen is whether he can consolidate his new base – and turn the radical right as the main force in the land.

This is, indeed, the key question facing Italian politics, increasingly cohered into a binary of *salviniani* and their opponents. This was apparent in August 2019, as Salvini decided the time had come to cash in his lead in the polls – and swat away even the feeble constraints placed on him by M5S's presence in government. With the right-wing bloc well over 50 per cent in the polls – and the Lega now the nation's biggest party, after victory in the European elections – he announced his resignation from the Interior Ministry, as he sought to force the fresh elections that would bring him to the prime minister's office. Yet the ever-successful Salvini here encountered a first setback. Where it was in Salvini's interest to go to the polls, the M5S entered into self-preservation mode: founder Beppe Grillo wrote a blog post invoking the 'consistency of the cockroach', and the need for compromise when 'barbarians [were] at the gates'.[21] For Matteo Renzi, too, it was time to stop sitting back with the popcorn – and help broker a new alliance between the M5S, the PD and his own personal allies. Salvini had, once again, succeeded in uniting an apparently unnatural set of forces. Yet this time around, they were attempting to block him – the once-anti-establishment M5S, now entering the embrace of the nation's leading centrist party. They hoped, at least, that they could keep the barbarians at the gates – if only for a few years more.

Conclusion

As I put the finishing touches to this book in late January 2020, the Democratic Party was celebrating its election victory in Emilia-Romagna – one of a handful of enduring red fortresses. After the formation of the PD–M5S coalition in September 2019 the Lega had continued its electoral advance – in this contest Salvini promised that a win for his candidate would give the final 'shove' to the government. In the end, he was defeated, as the centre-left won with 51.4 per cent of the vote. In an op-ed for *La Repubblica* Massimo Giannini could proclaim that 'Stalingrad has not fallen'.[1] Anti-fascist metaphors had repeatedly surfaced during the campaign itself; thousands of anti-Lega protesters had gathered at sites like Bologna's Piazza Maggiore, singing the Resistance anthem *Bella Ciao* and declaring themselves the 'partisans for 2020'.[2] So named for the way they packed into city squares, these 'Sardines' claimed a non-partisan, democratic inspiration, and were widely credited with mobilizing the vote against Salvini in the historic anti-fascist heartland.

As election results trickled in, PD leader Nicola Zingaretti offered his 'immense thanks to the Sardines' for the mass turnout for the centre-left candidate.

The PD's relief over the result was striking. This was, after all, a stronghold that the Left would once have thought unassailable. Romagna was home to Italy's first socialist party back in 1881, it was a mainstay of the Resistance against fascism, and from 1970 the Communist Party and its successors retained uninterrupted control, building a dense associative web linking party to cooperatives, unions and municipalised companies. The withering of such structures has had clear electoral effects – in 2019 the PD lost mayoralties like Ferrara and Forlì to the Lega, and then the previously impregnable regional government in Umbria. These defeats did not so much suggest that PD voters were decamping to the Lega, as that popular demoralisation had allowed the Right to sneak in on a low turnout. In the end, the polarised campaign in Emilia-Romagna helped the PD scrape home: the 1 million votes for Salvini's candidate almost matched the total that Berlusconi had racked up in 2000, but enough of the centre-left's base turned out to deny him.

The election thus saw a hardening polarisation between centre-left and the populist right – perhaps pointing even to a fresh recomposition of the party system. Within the right-wing bloc, support overwhelmingly flowed toward Salvini's party: where the Lega candidate took 32 per cent of the vote, Berlusconi's Forza Italia vehicle was reduced to a meagre 2.6 per cent – trailing behind the postfascist Giorgia Meloni's Fratelli d'Italia, on 8.6 per cent. The Right's total number of votes was not a historic high, even in this 'red region' – but these voters had swung behind increasingly radical forces. The PD endeavoured to centre the election on local issues, from kindergartens to free school transport. But the Lega's own culture-warrior approach – whipping up scandal over the adoption of children by social services, and indeed the recent parole of a child-killer – showed the power of a stridently populist agenda, not directly centred on material demands but rather the radical delegitimisation of the left.

Yet this polarisation mainly owed to a less-noted aspect of the election – the effective demise of the party that had first lifted Salvini into national government. Even as the Five Star Movement remained the largest single force in parliament, indeed the party with the strongest representation in national government, it slumped to pitiful results, as its voters polarised between the PD candidate (taking two-thirds of their votes)[3] and, in lesser measure, the Lega. Back in the March 2018 general election, the M5S had been the largest single party in Emilia-Romagna, with 27.5 per cent support – this time, it slumped to 4.7 per cent. In a simultaneous contest in Calabria, in the M5S's southern heartlands, there was an even more precipitous fall, from 43.4 per cent to 6.2 per cent in under two years. While regional contests have often been unkind to M5S, there was no hiding the sense of crisis. With the party stumbling in the polls, leader Luigi di Maio resigned four days before the elections even took place.

At the time of writing, the M5S was still in government, together with the PD. Yet with such poor results – and poll ratings at under half its 2018 score – this 'anti-establishment' force now appears as a parliamentary rump, terrified of the next encounter with the electorate. Such a rapid decline well illustrates M5S's fundamental shallowness, unable to meet the test of institutional power. Having promised never to enter coalitions, within eighteen months of its March 2018 election win it had allied first with the Lega, then with the Democrats, in each case becoming the subordinate partner despite its greatly larger number of MPs and senators. Before his death in 2016, co-founder Gianroberto Casaleggio had insisted the M5S would govern with the PD 'over my dead body': this did, indeed, come to pass, exposing its full incoherence. Rather than change the forms of politics, the M5S was itself changed, throwing overboard first its anti-corruption charter, then its no-coalition policy, then its commitment to strip press barons of state funding.

Such a dismal story fits well with the political times explored in this book – an intense volatility, borne of the disconnect between ephemeral party containers and a fragmented Italian society. In chapters 1 and 5, we saw the contingent events which facilitated Salvini's rise – from the downfall of Bossi to the final conviction of Berlusconi and the M5S's willingness to lift him to the Interior Ministry. This success was, however, also based on deeper strengths of the Lega, whose deep-rooted territorial organisation has time and again allowed it to survive temporary electoral setbacks. Raised to national government in June 2018, Salvini used his media platform to swallow up his right-wing brother-enemies, making the Interior Ministry into the stage for a permanent election campaign. When, in August 2019, he attempted to cash in his successes – splitting the M5S–Lega coalition – he did not get the early elections he was looking for. Yet by all indicators the M5S is a party living on borrowed time, whereas Salvini heads a right-wing bloc commanding over 50 per cent in the polls.

Italian politics defy easy predictions, and Salvini's bid for an enduring hegemony still has hurdles to clear. The Lega's territorial organisation in the South is relatively shallow, whereas the post-fascist Fratelli d'Italia is currently a rising force – factors which at least pose problems to his bid to turn his poll lead and media platform into a genuinely national party. The boasts of looming victory in Emilia-Romagna, like the failed bid for early elections, have perhaps gone some way to dent his credibility as a winner. Yet the generational shift from the Berlusconi-era *centrodestra* to the nationalist right led by Salvini represents a formidable and lasting enemy for the left – the Lega's recently won mayors and regional offices should allow the extension of its hegemony and the deepening of its organisation. And as in the days of anti-Berlusconism, purely defensive responses – the moral call to rally all forces against Salvini, to stop the 'barbarians at the gates' – risk merely feeding his bid to polarise the political field around his own chosen themes.

If Emilia-Romagna was, indeed, a 'Stalingrad', it seems far from clear that the heirs of Italian Communist Party will do more than defend their last fortresses – and actually go on to reconquer lost ground. With the PD's defeat in Calabria, the same day as the Emilia-Romagna vote, the centre-left was reduced to control of just six regions, as against thirteen for the right. But more fundamentally, the class profile of PD voters, increasingly based upon the wealthiest and oldest Italians, points to a dismal future – a party no longer able to promise better days ahead, instead begging its former base to hold back the hordes. The ongoing collapse of the M5S heralds the return of a traditional polarisation, setting the centre-left bloc in opposition to the right led by Salvini's Lega. Yet what has changed is the content of these blocs – for the centre left no longer appears a vehicle able to galvanise working people in the cause of greater material well-being and deeper democratic participation.

This book was also finished at a decisive moment in European politics, as the United Kingdom left the European Union. Since the Brexit vote in June 2016, the prospect of other countries following it out the door – perhaps including an Italexit or Italeave – has continually decreased. If press suggested in the build-up to the March 2018 Italian general election that the election of a populist coalition might herald a fresh crisis event for the euro, both the Lega and M5S had already abandoned calls for a referendum on exit, and their short-lived opposition to Brussels' budget restraints proved purely theatrical. Forming a stronger hard-right bloc in the European Parliament in May 2019, Salvini has voiced his base's own Euroscepticism, but mainly on the grounds of immigration and what Brussels euphemistically calls 'preserving the European way of life'. This does not mean that Italy's difficult relationship with European integration has found an answer – or that the Lega in opposition will refrain from damning fiscal constraints like the European Stability Mechanism.

Since the signing of the Maastricht Treaty in 1992, an event which followed soon after the dissolution of the Communist Party, the centre-left has continually asserted the primacy of European rules over all other considerations – embracing the 'external bind' on Italian democratic politics. This has, as in other countries, provided an ideological framing for the left's weakened roots in class politics, not showing that Europe can provide material benefits for working people so much as demanding sacrifices from these latter in the name of Europeanism. For want of any perspective for reversing the terms of this relationship – securing relief from the mountain of debt or achieving the space to borrow and invest – the only effect can be a continued hollowing out of the left's social base, reduced to a few holdouts comfortably enough off to treat the European question as a culture war alone. It is true that the working class does not look like it once did – but the Italian centre-left isn't mobilising the precarious, the pink-collar or self-employed, either.

It would be optimistic to say that Italy finds itself at the crossroads, as if choosing between two different paths – for if the tumult of Italian politics defies easy predictions, the Lega is by far the most dynamic force, with the clearest opportunities to sink roots. A continued lack of economic growth, and the dangers posed by the next crisis in the eurozone, seem much more likely to feed the Lega's nationalism, even if this does not imply any outright break with the EU project. The prospects of a left-wing alternative remain bleak: for almost three decades this very project has served as the ideological framing for what Luciano Gallino calls the 'class struggle after the class struggle',[4] namely the war on social and labour rights, the upward redistribution of wealth, and the slashed public investment that have followed the near-total collapse of the old Left and the workers' movement. Among all European countries, these forces are perhaps weaker in Italy than anywhere else.

For Salvini, like Berlusconi in his heyday, the war on the left – on 'reds' and 'communists' – can continue, even in the absence of organised communist forces. Posed as redemption from the left's supposed cultural dominance, this allows a harsh nationalism to be posed in the terms of victimhood, not unlike the far-right populisms spreading across central and eastern Europe. Like in Viktor Orbán's Hungary or Poland under Law and Justice, the delegitimisation of the left is being used to demand the silence of a much wider array of oppositional forces, from NGOs working on migrant rescue to feminists and environmentalists. Yet defending such movements is but one part of the vast challenges that face a paralysed Italian left. After decades of defeats, what it most of all lacks is the ability to imagine itself as more than a force of resistance, opposition and subculture – one able to mobilise the social majority, conquer institutions and use them to mount a wider revitalisation of the Italian economy and society.

In Gallino's terms, the loss of collective hope – the belief that common actions can have a real bearing on political and economic decisions – has given rise to individual and atom-ised responses, characterised by disillusionment and despair. These have been the sentiments mobilised by both the Five Star Movement and the Lega, in turn planting their flags in former heartlands of the Left. The socialists used to speak of the 'sun of the future', the promise of tomorrow – a vision hard to imagine in the current climate. Deprived of a party of their own, the atomised masses have broken up into disempowered fragments, capable of sporadic signs of discontent but not to carry forth an alternative set of values, a vision of regeneration, a community built on collective pride. Italy does, indeed, have social conflict, but it is a war being fought from above, dismantling and disaggregating the historic conquests of the labour movement and driving an ever-harsher climate of resentment, division and disdain for the public sphere.

I started this book saying that Italy is not such an outlier – in fact, it's more like a concentration of the present condi-tion, than a throwback to the past. For all the unfamiliarity of its party acronyms and all the idiosyncrasies of its regions, Italy has in recent decades served as a laboratory for changes which we now see spreading across the West. The recasting of the right by a nationalist demagogue, and indeed the collapse of the working-class left, are hardly phenomena limited to this peninsula; the wider weakening of political engagement and democratic institutions are, similarly, becoming increasingly apparent even beyond Italian shores. Here, as elsewhere, defiant campaigns for the lesser evil, rallying all forces to keep the 'barbarians' at bay, never seems to stop the evils from getting worse. Liberal press used to complain that the vulgar populist Berlusconi was undermining Italian public life – and that the tycoon's all-dominant position would never end. Now, as Italy's political meltdown continues apace, some would be glad to have him back.[5]

For Salvini's opponents, calling him a liar, corrupt, and a fascist has not yet opened up a breach in his support. Yet worse, it shows perilously little sign of giving the social majority a sense that politics can improve their lives – and that there's more to political action than keeping the barbarians at bay. For three decades the left has been unable to answer that problem, and not only on this peninsula. Doing so is an imperative, before we all find that Italy is a mirror of our own futures.

Acknowledgements

When I first lived in Rome in summer 2011, to do archival research on my undergrad history thesis, I would not have imagined that my life would become so bound to Italy. The near death of the Italian left has, at least, made for interesting times. But the writing of this book was also enlivened by friends met along the way, some of whom were kind enough to read drafts of chapters. No discredit attaches to them on account of more polemical parts of my text.

In no particular order I would like to thank Luca Cangianti, Lorenzo Alfano, Lorenzo Zamponi, Ornella Punzo, Martina Caruso, Simone Gasperin, Giacomo Gabbuti, Thomas Fazi, Bethan Bowett-Jones, Marta Fana, Loren Balhorn and, indeed, Julia Damphouse. Thanks also to the staff at Bar Marani, from whose terrace I wrote most of this text, and all at Verso Books, in particular Sebastian Budgen.

Notes

1 The Pole of Good Government

1 Eugenio Salvati and Michelangelo Vercesi, 'Party Organizations and Legislative Turnover: Signals of an Unstable Parliamentary Class?', *Italian Political Science*, 13, 1, May 2018.

2 This widely used expression seems to have appeared first in 'The Wills of the People', *The Economist*, 17 May 2018.

3 Cited by Simonetta Fiori in 'Alberto Asor Rosa: "Dobbiamo recuperare il senso di superiorità"', *La Repubblica*, 24 August 2013.

4 Cited in RJB Bosworth, *Mussolini's Italy: Life under the Fascist Dictatorship, 1915–1945*, Penguin, London, 2007, 543.

5 Paolo Mieli, *Il caos italiano*, Milan: Rizzoli, 2017.

6 See the interview with Cossiga on these outbursts: 'Cossiga vent'anni dopo le picconate "Potessi tornare indietro starei zitto"', *Corriere della Sera*, 2 August 2009.

7 Citied in Gianni Barbacetto, 'L'inchiesta vecchio stile Mani pulite, anno zero', *Archivio '900*, 15 February 2002.

8 Antonio Gibelli, *26 gennaio 1994*, Bari, Laterza, 2019.

9 'Berlusconi scende in campo – 1994', video at youtube.com/watch?v=3OlQ762Qh-A.

10 Ibid.

11 So named after its author Sergio Mattarella, a Christian Democrat who

later joined the Democratic Party and from January 2015 served as president of the republic.

12 See my critical obituary of Pansa, 'The Fascists' Historian', *Jacobin*, 14 January 2020. For a study of his polemical style and evasive use of unsourced claims, see Gino Candreva, 'La Storiografia à la Carte di Giampaolo Pansa', *Zapruder*, June 2017.

13 Lucio Magri, *The Tailor of Ulm*, London: Verso Books, 2012, 45.

14 See Bruno Anastasia and Giuseppe Tattara, 'Come mai il Veneto è diventato così ricco? Tempi, forme e ragioni dello sviluppo di una regione di successo', MPRA Paper 18458, 9 November 2009.

15 Ilvo Diamanti, 'La Lega, imprenditore politico della crisi. Origini, crescita e successo delle leghe autonomiste in Italia', *Meridiana*, 16, 1993, 99–133.

16 Ibid., 111.

17 Guido Vergani, 'Il carrocccio che travolge i partiti', *La Repubblica*, 9 May 1990.

18 Mattia Madonia, 'Perché il sud sta votando in massa chi li chiamava terroni, ladri e fannulloni', *The Vision*, 31 May 2019.

19 Andrea Pannocchia and Susanna Ceccardi, *Il Popolo di Salvini, La Lega Nord fra vecchia e nuova militanza*, Massa: Eclettica Edizioni, 2016, 27.

20 Ibid., 21.

21 Ibid., 20.

22 Ibid., 15.

23 On the party's make-up see Gianluca Passarelli and Dario Tuorto, *La Lega di Salvini. Estrema destra di governo*, Bologna: il Mulino, 2019.

24 Daniele Albertazzi, 'Going, Going . . . Not Quite Gone Yet? "Bossi's Lega" and the Survival of the Mass Party', *Contemporary Italian Politics*, 8, 2, 2016, 115–30.

25 Gianluca Passarelli and Dario Tuorto, *La Lega di Salvini. Estrema destra di governo*, Bologna: il Mulino, 2018, 45.

26 This relationship is interestingly discussed in Jonathan Hopkin, 'New Parties in Government in Italy: Comparing Lega Nord and Forza Italia', ECPR Joint Sessions, April 2004.

27 'Bossi: "Pronti a trascinare il popolo"', *Corriere della sera*, 7 October 2009.

2 'Say Something Left-wing!'

1 Peter Mair, *Ruling the Void: The Hollowing of Western Democracy*, London: Verso Books, 2013.

2 Centro Italiano Studi Elettorali, 'Il ritorno del voto di classe, ma al contrario (ovvero: se il PD è il partito delle élite)'.

3 In the previous contest in 1948 it had stood as part of a joint list together with the Socialists: this was thus the first postwar general election at which the PCI scored a representative tally. It was also an advance on its vote in the 1946 Constituent Assembly election, where it took 19 per cent.

4 Stathis Kouvelakis, 'Syriza's Rise and Fall', *New Left Review*, II, 97, January–February 2016, 45–70.

5 Max Jäggi, et al., *Red Bologna*, London: Writers and Readers Publishing Cooperative, 1977.

6 Pier Paolo Pasolini, 'Io so', *Corriere della Sera*, 14 November 1974.

7 Ibid.

8 Francesco Cattabrini, 'Franco Modigliani and the Italian Left-wing: The Debate over Labor Cost (1975–1978)', *History of Economic Thought and Policy*, 2012, 1, 75–95.

9 Ibid.

10 Guido Liguori, *La morte del PCI*, Roma: manifestolibri, 2009, 10. I was pointed to this section by Thomas Fazi and William Mitchell, *Sovranità o barbarie. Il ritorno della questione nazionale*, Milan: Meltemi, 2018, 96.

11 'Dove va il Pci', *La Repubblica*, 28 July 1981.

12 Lucio Magri, *The Tailor of Ulm*, London: Verso, 2012.

13 On this party's history, see my interview with Fulvio Lorefice, 'Italy's Past Glories', *Jacobin Magazine*, 28 February 2018; in Italian, see Fulvio Lorefice, *Ribellarsi non basta I subalterni e l'organizzazione necessari*, Rome: Bordeaux Edizioni, 2017.

14 Giacomo Gabbuti, 'Vento d'estate', *Jacobin Italia*, 12 August 2019.

15 See, for example, Alessandro Speciale and Chiara Albanese, 'Is the Euro to Blame for Italy's Economic Woes?', *Bloomberg Businessweek*, 18 December 2018.

16 Jeremy Gaunt, 'Two Reasons Why Italians Are Turning Sour on the Euro', *Reuters*, 12 April 2017.

17 Fazi and Mitchell, *Sovranità o Barbarie*, 105–8.

18 Ibid.

19 Cédric Durand, 'The Workers Have No Europe', *Catalyst*, Winter 2018.

20 See Tristan Auvray and Cédric Durand, 'A European Capitalism? Revisiting the Mandel-Poulantzas Debate', in *The End of the Democratic State*, London: Palgrave Macmillan, 2018, especially 155–65.

21 As he put it, the system's fundamental problem from an Italian perspective is that 'Not only is the pivot currency of the system fundamentally undervalued, but the growth of domestic demand in [West] Germany

is lower than average'. Quoted in Christina R. Sevilla, 'Explaining the September 1992 ERM Crisis: The Maastricht Bargain and Domestic Politics in Germany, France, and Britain', paper presented at the European Community Studies Association, Fourth Biennial International Conference, 11–14 May 1995, 8.

22 Fazi and Mitchell, *Sovranità o barbarie*.

23 See the interesting comments in Joseph Halevi, 'Europa e "Mezzogiorni"', *Palermograd*, 21 April 2016.

24 Mario Monti, *Intervista sull'Italia in Europa*, Bari: Laterza, 1998, 40, 176.

25 See the historical trend at tradingeconomics.com/italy/government-debt-to-gdp.

26 Romano Prodi, *Governare l'Italia. Manifesto per il cambiamento*, Rome: Donzelli, 1995, 12–18.

27 'Prodi: "Diciotto mesi di tagli e sacrifici per guarire l'Italia"', *La Repubblica*, 30 April 1996.

28 'Intervento del Presidente della Repubblica Carlo Azeglio Ciampi in occasione della cerimonia celebrativa dell'immissione in circolazione dell'euro, 26 November 2001,' available at presidenti.quirinale.it.

29 Giorgio Napolitano, *Europa politica. Il difficile approdo di un lungo percorso*, Rome: Donzelli, 2003, 12.

30 Claire Guyot, 'Italy: From Pro-European to Euroscepticism', euractiv.fr, 13 March 2018. Citing a policy paper by the Institut Jacques Delors, Guyot remarks: 'In 1991, 79 per cent of Italians expressed favourable opinions about their country's membership of the bloc compared to only 36 per cent in autumn 2017 (41 per cent had a neutral viewpoint).'

3 A Country for Old Men

1 'La provocazione del viceministro Martone: Laurearsi dopo i 28 anni è da sfigati', *La Repubblica*, 24 January 2012.

2 Enrico Pugliese, *Quelli che se ne vanno*, Bologna: il Mulino, 2018.

3 Hannah Roberts, 'Italian Miner Takes 35 Years' Sick Leave Because He's CLAUSTROPHOBIC – Then Retires on Full Pension', *Daily Mail*, 21 October 2014.

4 Thomas Fazi and William Mitchell, *Sovranità o barbarie. Il ritorno della questione nazionale*, Milan: Meltemi, 2018, 226–27.

5 'Lavoro: per il 50 per cent dei giovani assunti il primo contratto è a tempo determinato', *SIR*, 25 February 2019, commenting on the ISTAT report *Il mercato del lavoro 2018. Verso una lettura integrata*.

6 'Fareed Zakaria GPS – Mario Monti, Prime Minister, Italy', CNN, 18 May 2012, available at youtube.com/watch?v=peac2sZXWvs.

7 'Di Maio: nel Def ci sarà un capitolo famiglia', *Vita*, 2 April 2019.

8 'Davvero in Italia ci sono più pensionati che lavoratori?', *Agi*, 29 June 2019.

9 Ibid.

10 'L'Europa del lavoro: nel 2017 tasso di occupazione (20-64 anni) al 72,2 per cent. Italia staccata di 10 punti si ferma al 62,3 per cent. I dati Eurostat', *Quotidiano Sanità*, 1 May 2018.

11 'Abbiamo le prove: l'occupazione femminile cresce grazie agli asili nido', *Linkiesta*, 28 June 2019.

12 Cited in Nadia Somma, 'Donne, guadagnano meno degli uomini perché vivono in società fallocentriche', *Il Fatto Quotidiano*, 29 January 2018.

13 'Young Italian Workers Are among Worst Paid in Europe', thelocal.it, 17 February 2016.

14 A phrase that made the title of Philip Mirowski's 2013 book *Never Let a Serious Crisis Go to Waste: How Neoliberalism Survived the Financial Meltdown*, London: Verso.

15 'ECB Letter Shows Pressure on Berlusconi', *Financial Times*, 29 September 2011.

16 The letter is reproduced at 'Dear Prime Minister', *Jacobin*, 27 November 2018.

17 Ibid.

18 In 'abrogative' referendums of this kind, launched by popular initiative, a 50 per cent turnout is a condition of the referendum counting. Thus, the most effective tactic for opponents of the intended policy (in this case, stopping privatisation) is to not vote at all. The scale of this vote as well as three others the same day, however, illustrated the strength of popular feeling.

19 See the reconstruction of these events in Perry Anderson, 'The Italian Disaster', *London Review of Books*, 21 May 2014.

20 Giacomo Vaciago, 'La lettera da Francoforte che ha cambiato l'Italia', *Il Sole 24 Ore*, 3 August 2012.

21 'Democracy's Conundrum: Reforms Take Time to Mature – But Voters Want Results Now', *Huffington Post*, 13 May 2014.

22 Paolo Decrestina, 'Disoccupazione, Berlusconi: "I giovani si svegliano a mezzogiorno e la sera vanno in discoteca"', *Corriere della Sera*, 14 February 2018.

23 According to ISTAT statistics: see 'Jobs act: quali effetti ha avuto sul mercato del lavoro? L'analisi', *QuiFinanza*, 20 December 2018. The

analysis discussed in this article was based on a study by two economists sympathetic to Renzi.

24 Marta Fana, *Non è lavoro è sfruttamento*, Bari: Laterza 2019, 408.

25 Ibid, 406.

26 Ibid, 1101.

27 Giuliano Balestreri, "Il lavoro è un'opportunità per chi ama la bici', ma soprattutto per i conti di Foodora', *La Repubblica*, 8 October 2016.

28 Riccardo Realfonzo and Guido Tortorella Esposito, 'Gli insuccessi nella liberalizzazione del lavoro a termine', *Economia e Politica*, 13 May 2014.

29 *OECD Employment Outlook 2016*, available at oecd-ilibrary.org.

30 C. J. Lasinio and G. Vallanti, *Reforms, Labour Market Functioning and Productivity Dynamics: A Sectoral Analysis for Italy*, MEF Working Papers no. 10, September 2013, cited by Fazi and Mitchell, *Sovranità o barbarie,* 227.

31 According to the 2016 Willis Towers Watson *Global 50 Remuneration Planning Report*, as cited in 'Young Italian Workers Are among Worst Paid in Europe', thelocal.it, 17 February 2016.

32 Simone Gasperin, 'Riuscire a riveder le stelle? Uno sguardo al passato per un Rinascimento economico italiano', in *I giovani salveranno l'Italia. Come sbarazzarsi delle oligarchie e riprenderci il futuro,* ed. Samuele Mazzolini, Reggio Emilia: Imprimatur, 2018.

33 Marta Fana, *Non è lavoro è sfruttamento*, Bari: Laterza, 2019, 1342.

34 Banca d'Italia, *Productivity Growth in Italy: A Tale of a Slow-motion Change*, Occasional Paper no. 422, January 2018.

35 Note the remarkable blanket condemnation of building new infrastructure in Roberto Bui, 'Non c'è lotta al negazionismo climatico senza lotta contro le 'grandi opere'', *Jacobin Italia*, 27 August 2019. For a different perspective, see Simone Gasperin, 'Autostrade ai privati. Come invertire la marcia', *Jacobin Italia*, 13 November 2018.

36 I analyse the politics of infrastructure spending cuts in 'L'Italia non regge', *Internazionale*, 24 August 2018, in English as 'Hanging Over the Edge', *Jacobin*, 17 August 2018.

4 Send in the Clowns

1 Bruno Amable and Stefano Palombarini, 'The Bloc Bourgeois in France and Italy', in *Economic Crises and Policy Regimes*, ed. Hideko Magara, London: Edward Elgar, 2014, 177–216.

2 Stefano Palombarini, 'Il liberismo autoritario', *Jacobin Italia*, 25 July 2019.

3 'A Bizarre New Government Takes Shape in Italy', *The Economist*, May 24 2018. This article similarly referred to Europe's 'first all-populist coalition'.

4 Marco Revelli, *The New Populism: Democracy Stares into the Abyss*, London: Verso, 2019, 163–95.

5 Andrea Carugati, 'M5S come il Pci di Berlinguer, al Sud ha conquistato i proletari', *La Stampa*, 6 March 2018.

6 This theme is interestingly addressed in Michael J. Sodaro, 'The Italian Communists and the Politics of Austerity', *Studies in Comparative Communism*, 13, 2–3, 1980, 220–49.

7 Only a short clip of this 2009 intervention is still available online, in later articles sarcastically remarking on Fassino's 'prophesy': see, for instance, 'La prima profezia di Fassino: "Grillo fondi un partito, vediamo quanti voti prende"', *La Repubblica*, 12 May 2015.

8 Dario Fo, Gianroberto Casaleggio, and Beppe Grillo, *Il Grillo canta sempre al tramonto*, Milan: Chiarelettere, 2013.

9 'Italy's Beppe Grillo: Meet the Rogue Comedian Turned Kingmaker', *TIME*, March 7 2013.

10 Ibid.

11 'Grillo ai militanti di Casa Pound: Il leader M5S davanti al Viminale', *La Stampa*, 11 January 2013.

12 'Grillo: "Eliminiamo i sindacati, voglio uno Stato con le palle"', *La Repubblica*, 18 January 2013.

13 For an interesting analysis of Podemos's 'non-party' identity, see Manuel Cervera-Marzal, 'Podemos: A "Party-Movement" in Government', *Jacobin*, 9 January 2020. Comparisons between M5S and Podemos include Christopher Bickerton and Carlo Invernizzi Accetti, '"Techno-populism" as a New Party Family: The Case of the Five Star Movement and Podemos', *Contemporary Italian Politics*, 10, 2, 2018, 132–50, and Paolo Gerbaudo, 'Are Digital Parties More Democratic Than Traditional Parties? Evaluating Podemos and Movimento 5 Stelle's Online Decision-making Platforms', *Party Politics*, 2019.

14 Beppe Grillo, 'Tsunami Tour', beppegrilloblog.it, 11 January 2013.

15 Beppe Grillo, 'Gli italiani non votano mai a caso', beppegrilloblog.it, February 26 2013.

16 'Per Beppe Grillo: anziani pensionati e lavoratori pubblici = ladri', youtube.com/watch?v=ODjQ8j7fqeA.

17 'M5S, la versione di Casaleggio: '"Chi non mantiene gli impegni deve essere cacciato"', *Il Fatto Quotidiano*, 20 April 2014.

18 The minister who designed this reform in 2005, Roberto Calderoli, later deemed it a *porcata* (trash), leading it to receive this nickname – also a reference to the previous electoral law designed by Sergio Matarella, known as the *Mattarellum*.

19 '25 aprile: Napolitano lo esalta, per Grillo e' morto', *ANSA*, 25 April 2013.

20 Interestingly discussed in Revelli, *The New Populism*, 186.

21 As noted in Perry Anderson, 'The Italian Disaster', *London Review of Books*, 21 May 2014.

22 See Claudio Paudice, 'Tutte le gaffe di Ignazio Marino sindaco di Roma. Dal Panda-gate alla foto con Buzzi fino all'irritazione del Papa', *Huffington Post Italia*, 8 October 2015, as well as the further development of Marino's troubles with the Pope in 'Pope's Dislike of Rome Mayor Revealed in Prank Call on Radio Programme', *The Guardian*, 29 September 2015.

23 Alessandro di Battista, 'Smontare la Lega in 5 minuti', youtube.com/watch?v=Vr_ Sswb1jjA.

24 Ilvo Diamanti, 'La solitudine dei giovani elettori: ecco perché hanno votato No al referendum costituzionale', *La Repubblica*, 12 December 2016.

25 Jacopo Iacoboni, *L'Esperimento*, Bari: Laterza, 2018, 22.

26 'Gaia, the Future of Politics'. In heavily accented English at youtube.com/watch?v=sV8MwBXmewU.

27 'Grillo Ushers In Politics-for-Profit With Google Ads', *Bloomsberg*, 29 May 2013.

28 'M5S, Favia: '"Casaleggio prende per il culo tutti. Da noi la democrazia non esiste"', *Il Fatto Quotidiano*, 6 September 2012.

29 Iacoboni, *L'Esperimento*, 56.

5 Salvini's Triumph

1 Broder, 'Italy's Missing Euro Debate', *Jacobin*, 5 February 2018,

2 'Salvini a Palermo, parte la protesta "Toni eccessivi, mi scuso coi siciliani"', *Giornale di Sicilia*, 8 February 2015.

3 In the 2015 regional elections Noi con Salvini stood a handful of candidates, amassing under 40,000 votes across the South.

4 For repeated examples of this stretching from 2012 to 2015, see Matteo Marini, 'Quando Salvini diceva "Mai più con Berlusconi"', wilditaly.it, 9 April 2015.

5 'Regioni non più rosse: ecco perché la sinistra sta perdendo le sue roccaforti storiche', *Linkiesta*, 29 October 2019; 'Italy's Salvini Triumphant in Left-Wing Stronghold of Umbria', BBC News, 28 October 2019; Nicholas Farrell, 'Salvini's Plan to Smash Italy's Red Wall', *Unherd*, 24 January 2020.

6 'Di Maio: "Con la Lega o con 'Liberi e Uguali'? Valuteremo dopo il voto"', ANSA, 31 December 2017.

7 Ilario Lombardo, 'Svolta a 5 Stelle per il governo: "Patto con il Pd senza Renzi"', *La Stampa*, 19 December 2017.

8 Matteo Renzi (@matteorenzi), 'Quello di Macerata è un atto razzista, ma non sono i pistoleri . . .', Twitter, 5 February 2018, twitter.com/matteorenzi/status/960465127945461760.

9 'Macerata, Minniti: "Ho fermato sbarchi perché avevo previsto Traini. Accordo con Libia? Patrimonio dell'Italia"', *Il Fatto Quotidiano*, 8 February 2018.

10 Piera Matteucci, 'Raid razzista a Macerata, Salvini: "Colpa di chi ci riempie di clandestini". Renzi: "Ora calma e responsabilità"', *La Repubblica*, 3 March 2018.

11 Marco Conti, 'Migranti, Berlusconi: "Bomba sociale pronta a esplodere". Erdogan: "Spari a Macerata? È terrorismo"', *Il Mattino*, 4 February 2018.

12 Ipsos, 'Elezioni Politiche 2018. Analisi Post-Voto", March 2018, available at ipsos.com.

13 Fabio Martini, 'La scommessa vinta di Renzi: "E adesso pop-corn per tutti"', *La Stampa*, 10 May 2018.

14 Marco Damilano, 'La notte più buia della Repubblica e quei serpenti sulla Costituzione', *L'Espresso*, 27 May 2018, available at espresso.repubblica.it.

15 Jan Fleischhauer, 'Italien: Die Schnorrer vom Rom', *Der Spiegel*, 24 May 2018.

16 Matteo Pucciarelli, 'Salvini Ascendant', *New Left Review*, II, 116–17, 9–30.

17 Ibid, 25.

18 Ibid.

19 Susanna Turco, 'Pasticcieri, speaker radio, ex missini: ecco la Lega sudista (e riciclata)', *L'Espresso*, 24 September 2018.

20 Ibid.

21 Beppe Grillo, 'La coerenza dello scarafaggio', beppegrillo.it, 10 August 2019.

Conclusion

1 Massimo Giannini, 'Elezioni Regionali, Stalingrado non è caduta', *La Repubblica,* 27 January 2020.

2 'Sardine a piazza San Giovanni: "Siamo i partigiani del 2020"', *Adnkronos,* 14 December 2019; this referred to a demonstration in Rome, though Carlo Smuraglia, president of partisan veterans' association ANPI, himself drew parallels in an open letter to the Sardines on 3 December 2019, available at anpi.it.

3 'Claudio Bozza, Emilia-Romagna, la svolta degli elettori M5S: due su tre sono passati al Pd', *Corriere della Sera,* 27 January 2020.

4 Luciano Gallino, *La Lotta di Classe dopo la Lotta di Classe,* Bari: Laterza, 2012.

5 Bill Emmott, 'Italy's Sobering Election', 4 January 2018, *Project Syndicate.* Here, long-time Berlusconi critic and former *Economist* editor Bill Emmott said he would prefer the billionaire to a 'populist insurrection', on the grounds of stability.

Index